BREAKING THE
TIME BARRIER

THE TEMPORAL ENGINEERING OF SOFTWARE

For Advanced Engineers Only

GORDON E. MORRISON

Outskirts Press, Inc.
Denver, Colorado

Dedicated to

Catherine Morrison — confident, courageous, intelligent, independent, and self-sufficient. Thank you for your encouragement and understanding while I put this book together.

And

Ron Riedesel, a wonderful friend who brightened many of my days, and who was lost to all of us in the spring of 2008.

"This technique is so powerful and adaptive that it has the potential to be developed into a complete, model-driven architecture and holds the possibility of eliminating programmers as we know them."

Dr. Aynur Unal, Silicon Valley, 2005

Contents at a Glance

Preface

If you like academic works, avoid this book. I'm an inventor. If you like writing and debugging if-then-else code (spaghetti code), avoid this book. That's what I'm trying to get rid of. If you don't like spaghetti code, read on, learn of a cure to the common ailments that create spaghetti code.

Computer Aided Software Engineering (CASE) tools have failed in their design to eliminate spaghetti code. This design failure has resulted in CASE tools not making a solid connection between the model and the application. Until spaghetti code can be eliminated, CASE tools will remain under utilized. When approaches like CASE fail, the industry invents a new acronym and continues looking for a solution that will work. One of the new acronyms is MDA® (Model Driven Architecture). MDA is the new approach to computer-aided software engineering. Regardless of its name MDA shares the same fundamental problem of not being able to contain spaghetti code.

What will it take to make MDA work efficiently where others have failed? The answer is, the elimination of spaghetti code. Spaghetti code can be eliminated by managing the temporal component of software development and by keeping the control-flow separate from the data-flow. This approach allows the logic to be represented in a graphical display and to associate each logical transition with a behavior in order to manipulate data. A well-managed temporal component eliminates the problems caused by spaghetti code. Eliminating spaghetti code results in CASE tools able to manufacture code that can stay synchronized with the model. This book is the genesis of a revolution in temporal engineering and the decline of spatial theocracy.

The differences between temporal and spatial code can be understood using another form of architecture. If the architecture of an application is viewed as a skyscraper, the members, functions, or procedures are the offices. If a skyscraper were built with a spatial architecture, there will be no hallways or elevators. The path to an office will go through connecting offices; access to different floors will be through stairs connecting directly to an office on a different floor. A trace of the spatial paths visiting the offices will look like a pile of spaghetti.

A skyscraper built with a temporal architecture will have central elevators and hallways to provide direct access to offices throughout the building without traipsing through other offices. A trace of the temporal paths visiting the offices will look like the layout of the hallways and elevators.

As the title of the book suggests, this book is about the process of engineering temporal software. This is NOT the process currently called software engineering, which is primarily an administrative process. To engineer temporal software is a skill and discipline that can be repeated over and over. It is based on knowledge gained from proper mentoring and repeated reviews of one's skills. Temporal software is coherent from beginning to end, and is so coherent that the model *is* the application.

Temporal software engineering is a disruptive technology[1] because it greatly reduces size, complexity and thereby cost. With the cost to develop software at $10 to $100+ per line of code, reducing application size and complexity is extremely important to the corporate bottom line. When a temporal architecture is fully implemented it can reduce

---

[1] Moore, Geoffrey A., *Crossing the Chasm*, HarperCollins Publishers, 1999.

the size of applications up to 50% and reduce complexity by a factor of up to three times and yet maintain the same functions and features.

According to a report[2] produced in the Department of Commerce software sales reached about $180 billion in 2000 with a development staff of 697,000 software engineers and an additional 585,000 computer programmers producing ITE spaghetti code. According to the same report the bugs in this annual production of software cost the US economy an estimated $60 billion. The math is easy, it's time for a new approach to software development.

---

[2] Gregory Tassey, "The Economic Impacts of Inadequate Infrastructure for Software Testing", May 2002, National Institute of Standards and Technology.

About the Author

Gordon Morrison is an inventor and a consultant. He has developed real-time weather radar systems, invented the technology known today as multi-core and hyper-threading technology (U.S. Patent 4,847,755), developed extensive database systems, developed high-performance communications systems, and developed micro-code for animation. Gordon's main interest has been improving the quality of software and reducing complexity.

Acknowledgments

My life has been enriched with the conversations of many intelligent people. In so many ways they have guided me down this path. In countless hours of technical conversations they have helped me through this process. Many thanks to: Fred Inman, Dick Pankoski, Robert Wilhelm, Fred Gluck, Chris Brooks, Mike Bottomley, Bret Bowman, Jan Hauser, Dave Merritt, Dr. Aynur Anul, and Dr. Richard Balay. In addition, I have enjoyed my long relationship with IEEE *Computer* magazine for giving me a good background and for not solving the problems that I've enjoyed solving.

I would like to single out three people who have special skills that were beneficial to me: Dick Pankoski for his ability to organize my rambling thoughts early in my career, and Fred Inman and Robert Wilhelm for allowing and encouraging me to be creative.

I would like to thank Robert Nesmith for allowing me to stay on his boat while I finished writing this book.

1

Chapter 1 – The Problem

There are several material considerations missing from the practice of software engineering. For Software Development to be an engineering profession, we need a reproducible discipline[3] with the artistry refocused to a more useful place. The creativity is in the solution, not the use of the language. Software engineering needs a better way to test, trace, and debug software. Furthermore, it needs a clearly understood temporal component[4], and a robust ability to handle misuse with a high level of confidence. This book puts forth a solution to all of these needs. This is a simple solution that may initially be difficult to understand since it represents a substantial change[5] in thinking.

Seasoned computer science professionals understand why Dr. Brooks wrote about the lack of discipline in the software profession and Dr. Lee wrote about the temporal needs in software development. These individual papers are elegant proof of how intensely the computer science profession embodies the "cobbler's children" cliché. Both of these distinguished professors lament about the lack of discipline in an engineering science run by young artists. A lack of discipline has resulted in software managers unable to control projects[6].

A way of solving the discipline problem is to eliminate the programmer as art and create an art in solving problems. This can be done using a Model Driven Architecture

---

[3] Brooks, Frederick P. Jr., "Three Great Challenges for Half-Century Old Computer Science" – *Journal of the ACM,* Vol 50 No. 1 January 2003, pp 25-26.
[4] Lee, Edward A., "Absolutely Positively on Time," *IEEE Computer*, Editorial March 8, 2005.
[5] Ernst von Glaserfeld, "The Reluctance to Change a Way of Thinking*", Irish Journal of Psychology, 1988.
[6] Charette, Robert N., "Why software fails. We waste billions of dollars each year on entirely preventable mistakes," © 2005 *IEEE Computer*, September 2005, page 42.

(MDA®) to manufacture the application code. However, the MDA[7] approach has failed because of a lack of continuity between the model and the implementation, causing the process to be incoherent. "Often, once construction begins, the teams leave the model behind and never update it to reflect their changing conceptions of the project."[8] The current MDA approach has failed because it doesn't solve the fundamental problem of "spaghetti code" which in turn doesn't match any model. It is extremely difficult to model free-form language. And free-form language creates an unstable application that is costly to maintain. When an application's call-logic is modeled, and the free-form code is examined, it looks like a "pile of spaghetti" (see Appendix F).

Brooks' concerns and Lee's temporal request can both be met by keeping control-flow and data-flow sections separate. This orthogonal approach results in strongly specialized functional sections. This orthogonal section makes it *impossible* to create "spaghetti code" but doesn't prevent the creation of "spaghetti logic." Even bad logic is easier to debug when it has been separated from data manipulation. In a profession not known for its discipline, this will be a challenge, but it can be accomplished through the approach shown here. A principle assumption is that the reader has an advanced understanding of the "if-then-else" (ITE) constructs of traditional code. The ITE approach imbeds the manipulation of data with the logic. For example the construct:

"(if a > x) then (a = a + 1); else (a = a – 1);"

contains two control-flow paths and two data-flow paths combined. The Coherent Object System Architecture (COSA) approach to coding doesn't allow this combination to happen.

---

[7] MDA is a Registered Trademark of the Object Management Group, www.omg.org/mda/
[8] Mesevery, Thomas, Fenstemacher, Kurt, "Transforming Software Development: An MDA Road Map," © 2005 *IEEE Computer*, September 2005, page 52.

The Software Engineering Institute (SEI) of Carnegie Mellon University (CMU) used a state machine technology to produce a successful software engineering administrative process[9]. Having a known name helps market their process Team Software Process (TSP). But, the CMU-SEI Personal Software Process (PSP) lacks the thoroughness needed to create engineered software. The PSP uses throwaway state tables that produce non-orthogonal code, which takes us right back to an ITE approach, which results in undisciplined "spaghetti code".

The TSP and PSP processes are successful given their limited use, however, the administration and engineering are faulty due to a lack of coherence. The SEI website (http://www.sei.cmu.edu) shows an example of their state template (it looks like a spreadsheet form), which gets filled in by the analyst and eventually "discarded" as documentation that will get out of sync with the application.

---

[9] "Personal Software Process/Team Software Process," Sponsored by U.S. Department of Defense – © 2005 by CMU.

2

Chapter 2 – The COSA Solution

This book demonstrates COSA engineered software. This name was developed to indicate the coherence needed to move from a model to manufactured code and have both stay synchronized. The architectural structure presented in this book will transform the way problems and specifications are viewed. It will require a substantial change in thinking and discipline to avoid reverting to an ITE approach.

The initial example of how to use COSA will be shown with a five-function calculator and the operations of "+", "-", "*", "/", and "%". This example creates an application complex enough to show the fundamentals of temporal engineering. Where the logic of control-flow is separate from data-flow. This approach to application development is not limited to small applications and can be applied to significantly more complex applications. In other words, it is completely scalable. The temporal component forces the analyst/engineer to fully define each state in time. This will be more easily understood when examining the logic. The ITE approach doesn't consider time as part of its analysis; it only considers order and thereby an implicit notion of time. In the COSA implementation, time is an explicit component that moves with the control-flow logic.

The CMU-SEI (PSP) process mentioned in Chapter 1 lacks the thoroughness needed to create temporal software. PSP uses throwaway state tables that produce non-orthogonal code, resulting in undisciplined "spaghetti code" which is an ITE approach. COSA, on the other hand, starts with a grammar that leads to a table. COSA *keeps and extends these state tables* and builds the application around them. There is no waste with COSA. In addition to the specification the three essential parts of COSA are the engine, a rules table, and the supporting procedures.

An Overview of the COSA Engine

In his book, *Code Complete 2,* Steve McConnell[10] has an entire chapter on table-driven methods. He encourages the use of table-driven methods for reducing the complexity of processing data. COSA expands on the initial table-driven approach to focus on reducing the complexity of logic.

COSA is based on an engine paradigm that uses time to reduce complexity through control-flow rules in a table that contains pointers to data-flow procedures. The complexity doesn't go away as the result of *magic*. The complexity is replaced with temporal logic managed by the engine.

The engine consists of the following:

```
0 Interface Name (Attributes if any)
1 Engine Control - While Scope used for preempting an object (real-time control)
2        Testing  - If managing logic analysis TRUE or FALSE
3                True Trace - managing temporal flow for debugging
4                True Behaviors  - actions supporting the true logic
5                Next True Time   - temporal control on true logic
6                        OR       - Then logic
7                False Trace - managing temporal flow for debugging
8                False Behaviors  - actions supporting the false logic
9                Next False Time  - temporal control on false logic
10        End of Testing Scope
11 End of Control Scope
12 Return Value if any
```

---

[10] McConnell, Steve, *Code Complete 2*, Copyright © 2004 Microsoft Press, Chapter 18.

Line 0 is the interface to the engine; it passes information into the engine. Line 1 is the engine's local control. The local control is tested on every iteration through the engine and will preempt the engine if the local control is set to false. When control is critical, a global state can be added to the local engine control to create a global preemption. There was a time when hitting a <ctrl>-A could stop an application. With the development of spaghetti objects, as Dick Pankoski called them[11], that control is no longer available.

Line 2 of the engine is the only place in the entire application where the "if" logic is found. This line compares the incoming dynamic state with the static state in the table. If it's true, lines 3-5 are executed. If it's false, lines 7-9 are executed. The COSA engine's only function is to traverse through the logic. (When you get to Chapter 10 on the data parser, an interesting dilemma appears that begs for ITE logic to quickly solve the problem; instead the problem is solved with COSA, a clean temporal logic.)

Trace control for true behavior is at line 3, and trace control for false behavior is at line 7. These locations in the engine-control provide two points for the developer to analyze program behavior. In a traditional ITE application, several lines of code must be added to provide a tracing scope equivalent to these two lines of code. In the ITE approach to coding, there are no central locations in the logic, as can be found in COSA. Using the COSA approach to tracing dramatically reduces the problems of turning trace on/off and any potential side effects that may occur. For those engineers involved in medical, security, or government projects this is the ultimate software trace. Trace can be dynamic or static. Dynamic trace produces runtime application information. Static trace tracks the evolution of how code changes over time.

---

[11] Personal Conversation

6

The engine's true behavior is at line 4, and the engine's false behavior is at line 8. Both behaviors are dynamically bound to their respective columns in the control-flow logic table on each iteration of the engine. Dynamic binding creates huge amounts of flexibility limited only by one's imagination. The artistry lies solving the logic problems used in engineering software.

After a behavior has been executed, the engine retrieves the next temporal location for the true behavior at line 5 and for the false behavior at line 9. If the engine is still turned on after the respective behavior has been completed then it is ready for its next iteration.

An Overview of the COSA Rules Table

The COSA rules are contained in the rows of a table[12]. The COSA Rules Table has a dual nature that is both data and code. As data, the COSA Rules Table has the ability to change. As code, these data changes can represent a logic fix or the application changing as it learns new logic. The standard binary table in COSA has true and false logic in each row.

Regardless of the type of table implementation a row represents the temporal control-flow logic for the problem in a top-down progression of time. A row in the table represents what is expected of the problem and what to do when the expected results are received. A row in the table also represents what to do when the expected result is not received.

---

[11] "Agile Programming: Design to Accommodate," IEEE *Software* May/June 2005, Dave Thomas.

The columns have specific relationships to the structure of the engine. Because most COSA tables represent binary behavior, errors in logic and operation are covered by default. This is not true in the traditional ITE approach, which requires the programmer to define a contrary action. By its very definition, the binary approach used by COSA is robust beyond anything that can be achieved by the ITE approach or the State Templates used by SEI.

> Recall from the preface that a skyscraper designed with ITE architecture doesn't have elevators or hallways. To do work "Control" dispatches a "runner" on a path, in one scenario. Since paths go through connecting offices imagine the problem of communicating an error back to control. The path would have to go through all of the previous offices to get back to control to correct the problem. Finally, the runner must return through a multitude of offices to the original location where the error was encountered.

> The temporal skyscraper model has elevators and hallways. The runner would simply leave the room where the problem occurred, walk down the hallway to control, correct the problem, and walk back to the appropriate office and continue working.

An Overview of the COSA Procedures

The procedures, as defined by COSA, execute one action specific to a behavior. There are times when the specific action is to do nothing because the procedure is a placeholder in the logic. When the action is complete the procedures participate in setting the correct dynamic state based on one specific action, if necessary.

An Overview of COSA Framework

Figure 2.0 shows an abstraction of a data migration application containing eight COSA objects. Each object consists of an engine, control-flow (Tables), and data-flow (Procedures).

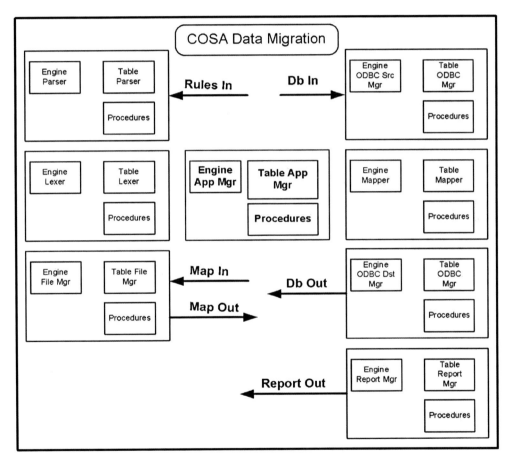

Figure 2.0
Abstraction of COSA Application

9

Summary

This book shows how COSA fills in the missing piece between the model and the application. The COSA approach to engineered software uses one or more engines as the central point of control. The control-flow is separated from data-flow, and all of the logic is in a coherent table, with simple coherent procedures. The COSA process eliminates the ITE approach that creates spaghetti code.

COSA technology is scalable. COSA works well with object technology, existing multi-threaded frameworks, or in procedural languages where embedded real-time performance, preemption, and predictability are critical.

3

Chapter 3 – An Example Using BNF with COSA

The product we will build is a five-function calculator. We are going to put the logic of the calculator application together using a COSA Extended BNF. The application analyst put together the specification defining the product based on what the customer wants[13]. Analysts are people with experience in the business and know the specifics of what the business needs. If an analyst gave the same specification to ten equally competent software engineers, then ten different designs would be received back. I have seen at least six different simple calculator designs, all work and each would be difficult to maintain because of the inherent complexity in the ITE approach. The differences in the implementation must be attributable to the interpretation of the specification. A high level of abstraction leaves much open to the developer to artistically create.

The Power of Using BNF

A powerful specification with a low level of abstraction can be created[14] with the use of Backus-Naur Form (BNF)[15]. Actually, the entire application can be created using a BNF structure. The Harvard Medical School in Boston started to create such a structure[16] for their internal use. It's one of many good examples of using BNF that can be found on the Internet.

---

[13] The requirements are the part that constrain and cannot be implemented.
[14] The industry needs a good integrated BNF editor and development tool.
[15] Backus, John, Dec 3, 1924- Mar 17, 2007, http://en.wikipedia.org/wiki/John_Backus
[16] "BNF and built-in classes for object-oriented guideline expression language (GELLO)," © 2001 Decision Systems Group, Omolola Ogunyemi, PhD, et al. aziz@dsg.harvard.edu

It's extremely important to remember that every computer language, every Internet GUI, every database, every protocol, and every user interaction passes through a BNF filter of some sort. BNF definitions are a very important place to start any new application. The following is a bit of BNF humor:

> A story is told about a language processing software that could translate technical English manuals into Russian. The Russians had software that could translate technical Russian manuals into English. Both applications were very good at these technical translations. It was decided to put some prose through these language translators. On the English side they put in *"The spirit is willing but the flesh is weak."* And sent it to the Russians. The Russians translated the prose back into English, which resulted in *"The ghost is ready but the meat is raw."*

An example will provide a better understanding of how COSA works. The idea for the calculator example comes from a book by Dr. Miro Samek, *Practical Statecharts in C/C++.*[17] The COSA example produces the same functionality as the ITE five-function calculator example in Samek's book. I refer to his book because of the excellent quality and thoroughness of his work in the spatial[18] domain. I appreciate Samek's "Quantum Programming" structures for advancing state machines. However, I believe COSA presents a better way of understanding logic using a temporal domain.

According to an SEI PowerPoint[19] presentation on their licensed software process, "designed programs are smaller" and "design takes longer" to create. The next step in

---

[17]Samek, Miro, PhD, *Practical Statecharts in C/C++,* State Diagram on pg 170, CMP Books, © 2002.
[18] See Preface for an introduction to spatial versus temporal softare.
[19] PSP II Designing and Verifying State Machines, PowerPoint Presentation, Copyright © 2005 Carnegie Mellon University.

designing a state machine, by the SEI approach, is to fill in the State Template. This will create all of the transitions among states and their respective actions taken within each state. Instead, we will take a structured language-based approach using BNF to create the logic. But, this approach is not based on a fixed BNF; instead we will be creating a dynamic BNF that will learn its domain-specific structure as the project develops.

To understand the control-flow logic in any application, a BNF approach, like the one described in this book, can be used. A BNF structure can also be used to describe and generate state diagrams, class diagrams, tree views, and a complete application. When the modeling tool maintains the underlying meta-data any change to the view represented by the tree diagram results in changes to the BNF and state diagrams. Consistency is maintained because the traditional "code" does not exist independent from the BNF definitions. Each section in the application is represented as BNF. Each section can be viewed as the analyst prefers because the underlying BNF creates the requested view. When every aspect of the project revolves around the BNF there is no need for the insertion of comments into a language to delineate computer-generated sections from human created sections of the application.

The Calculator Specification

We are provided with a complex operating system framework within which we will be building our product. Although, we have two user approaches we can implement, the user of our product is not an engineer and doesn't understand stacks, so we won't be building our use case based on reverse Polish notation like HP calculators. Instead, we will be using the TI® Algebraic Operating Systems approach where the user enters a number, then an operator, then enters a second number, and then clicks an equal key to get a result.

13

Our user would like to be able to correct entries and clear everything. Also, our user wants to use the second operand to calculate a percent of the first operand. The user only understands simple numbers with decimal points, nothing else. The framework provided by the platform will provide the GUI and real-time interaction. We will be providing the interface to the framework and the runtime behavior.

The form of the calculator is a Windows® application with buttons that can be clicked with a mouse to create an event that results in an action or behavior. The COSA approach is to start this application with a BNF[20] definition. The operational definition for the calculator is defined as four rules: rOper1 (100), rOper8 (500), rOper2 (700), and rResult (900). These operational rules are defined with the temporal component running from left to right and top down. The analyst chose the trace numbers associated with each rule, and they will be used for tracking the specification throughout the development process.

The rules all start with a lower case "r". Steps will be added to the rules to complete their definitions. These individual steps will become the states within the rules. Each state will start with a lower case "i".

Calculator   = <rOper1> <rOper8> <rOper2> <rResult>?;

In the BNF a vertical pipe "|" is used to allow for selecting between the different possibilities as in format A or format B. The less than and greater than symbols are used to contain and delineate symbol names that contain more than one word as in the <unary

[20] There is an international standard on Extended BNF "ISO/IEC 14977:1996(E)" called Information technology – Syntactic meta language – Extended BNF. I may or may not conform, but I will explain my usage to get my point across.

minus>. To simplify this kind of technical jargon I read these structures as "unary minus contained." As a brief reminder:

> Star "*" is used to define zero or more occurrences.
> Plus "+" is used to define one or more occurrences.
> Question "?" denotes zero or one occurrence for an optional argument.
> The listing <period> <digit> is the same as <period> THEN <digit>.
> Vertical Pipe "|" is used as a logical choice between productions.

(When I learned BNF in college, the production assignment was delineated by "::=". This always bothered me. In a temporal sense, once an assignment has been made, all that's needed is one symbol. There can be no ambiguity. But, until now, applications have developed BNF definitions in the ITE spatial domain where the parser doesn't keep track of time; they only keep track of states. We will look at this further when the explicit temporal component is introduced).

The first operand needs further definition. A number is defined as a collection of one or more digits ranging from zero through nine. Numbers can exist in several forms as positive numbers "+number", or as negative numbers "-number". Numbers can also have decimal portions containing a period followed by digits. The positive number is the default representation eliminating the need for the plus sign. The *acceptable* number formats for this calculator example are defined in three productions.

The ASCII values of the characters are used in the state name. The number 59 is the value for the period (decimal point) resulting in <iDot59> and is used to indicate the token's actual value when comparing the expected state to the dynamic state.

Number = <idigit>+ | <idigit>+ <iDot59> | <idigit>* < iDot59> <idigit>+;

It would be easy to expand on the definition of "Number" to include a production with plus or minus exponent limited to three digits.

Number2 = <idigit>+ <iDot59> <idigit>+ (<e> | <E>) (<+> | <->) <idigit>[3];

The specification says the Number2 format is not allowed, so we will keep this production in mind for more complex applications. Each rule can easily be expanded to include "features" that were not requested. However, part of the engineering discipline is to stay as close as possible to the specification without under providing or over providing. At some point the trace numbers will be assigned to each element in the BNF and tracked back to the specification. Upon design review the trace ability of COSA will help contain "feature creep" a well-known problem in the industry.

The first operand is then defined as an optional unary minus followed by the number definition. This definition of "Number" satisfies the requirements for entering a number at rOper1 and rOper2.

rOper1 = <iNeg44>? <Number>;

The operation is defined as the four functions that can be executed on the operands using the TI calculator style called AOS.

rOper8 = <iAdd43> | <iSub44> | <iMul42> | <iDiv47>;

The second operand is the same as the first operand and is defined as such.

rOper2 = <rOper1>;

16

The "Result" is more complex and is defined in terms of the percentage function and the equal sign.

The final "rResult" rule looks like the following:

rResult = <iPerc37> | <iEqual>;

The "Number" production has been reduced[21] to the most general format used by this calculator. The complete domain specific BNF for the calculator now looks like this:

Calculator	= <rOper1> <rOper8> <rOper2> <rResult>?;
rOper1 (100)	= <iNeg44>? <Number>;
Number	= <iDigit>* (<iDot59> <iDigit>+)?;
rOper8 (500)	= <iAdd43>	<iSub44>	<iMul42>	<iDiv47>;
rOper2 (700)	= <rOper1>;
rResult (900)	= <iPerc37>	<iEqual>;

BNF 3.0
COSA Calculator

Implicit in the BNF definition is time. Time flows from left to right and is connected through all of the rules. The explicit time component will be added later.

---

[21] Chapter 9 covers the advanced topics of "behavior reduction" and "behavior coalescence".

The Calculator Look and Feel

The calculator form is designed by dragging and dropping the various components from the Delphi Toolbar.

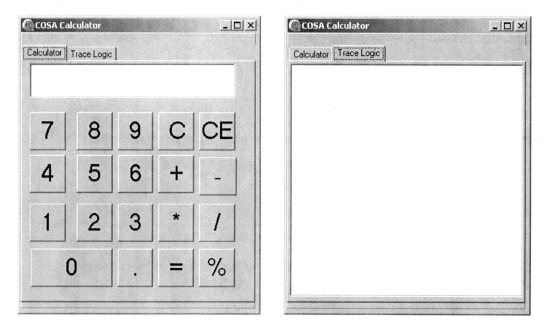

Figure 3.0
Calculator Form

Figure 3.1
Trace Logic Listbox

All of the labeled buttons have an associated "on-click" event. The display box in Figure 3.0 of the calculator doesn't have any associated click events. All of the button "on-click events call the calculator object "objCOSA" with their respective event data. The tab that says "Trace Logic" at the top contains a list box, shown in Figure 3.1, that displays trace/debug information. The above narrative, BNF, and the look and feel, complete the specification for the five-function calculator.

The Calculator Engine

The engine is the interface for the buttons' "on-click" events. The engine receives the tokenized value from each button's "on-click" event and a string containing the event type. The engine then compares the tokenized value of the dynamic state to the static state. If there is a match the true behavior is executed. If there isn't a match the false behavior is executed. The engine transitions according to the rules defined in the COSA Rules Table and respective procedures. When the rule is complete the engine is turned off and returns control to the Windows Message Loop.

The Calculator Rules Table

The Calculator's logic table consists of an array. In this example there are seven columns consisting of four pointers and three values. The specification has given the Rules Table four rule-sections. Section 100 covers the rules for the first operand. Section 500 covers the rules for the operators. Section 700 covers the rules for the second operand. Section 900 covers the rules for the results. The analyst chose the section numbers in the specification and will maintain these numbers throughout the design, development, and trace debugging.

The Calculator Procedures

The procedures are defined as coherent, which means they perform one simple function. They provide state information and turn the engine on or off as required by the rules. The try/except containment for the operator execution is the most complex procedure in the calculator. In special cases procedures are also used to instantiate, communicate, or access other objects depending on the structure of an application.

Summary

BNF is used to describe and generate diagrams, views, and applications that conform to COSA. The structured language-based approach that results from BNF is used to describe the logic. Once a BNF specification has been created it acts as the basis for representations throughout the application. The specification and BNF definitions were created for the calculator.

With the structure of the engine, control-flow table, and data-flow procedures fixed, the only true variables in COSA are the logic and the algorithms that manipulate the data. The structure remains consistent throughout COSA, like a software chip.

4

Chapter 4 – The COSA Rules Table in Detail

The previous chapter provided the fundamental BNF definition for the calculator. The four calculator rules were expanded into the steps necessary to perform the logic associated with the desired calculation of operating on two numbers and providing a result.

Calculator	= <rOper1> <rOper8> <rOper2> <rResult>?;
rOper1 (100)	= <iNeg44>? <Number>;
Number	= <idigit>* (<iDot59> <idigit>+)?;
rOper8 (500)	= <iAdd43> | <iSub44> | <iMul42> | <iDiv47>;
rOper2 (700)	= <rOper1>;
rResult (900)	= <iPerc37> | <iEqual>;

BNF 4.0
COSA Calculator

To make the detailed Rules Table for the calculator, the next step is to layout the domain specific BNF in a vertical tree structure. The four rules have steps that perform the necessary true or false behaviors[22] to complete that rule.

---

[22] When referring to an individual method in the table that method will be called an action. When referring to a method in a table from the engine's perspective, such as true or false, that member will be called a behavior because it is acting in temporal concert with other methods thereby creating a rule.

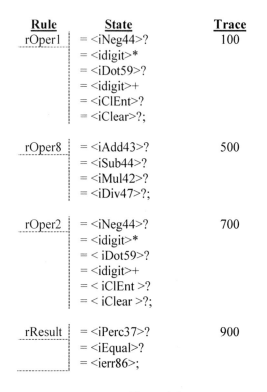

Rule	State	Trace
rOper1	= \<iNeg44\>?	100
	= \<idigit\>*	
	= \<iDot59\>?	
	= \<idigit\>+	
	= \<iClEnt\>?	
	= \<iClear\>?;	
rOper8	= \<iAdd43\>?	500
	= \<iSub44\>?	
	= \<iMul42\>?	
	= \<iDiv47\>?;	
rOper2	= \<iNeg44\>?	700
	= \<idigit\>*	
	= \< iDot59\>?	
	= \<idigit\>+	
	= \< iClEnt \>?	
	= \< iClear \>?;	
rResult	= \<iPerc37\>?	900
	= \<iEqual\>?	
	= \<ierr86\>;	

Tree 4.0
COSA Calculator BNF

The above tree structure is still missing the actions and the next temporal steps.

rOper1:

The tree structure needs actions added. Looking at Table 4.0 below, if the state in rule "rOper1" step \<iNeg44\> is true then we "Negate" the number. The calculator engine is turned off and control returns to the Windows Message Loop for the next behavior. If the entry isn't a minus sign, the false behavior "Ignore" is executed because the negating of a number is optional. Because the negating of a number is optional the false "Ignore" behavior doesn't turn the calculator engine off. In either case, time moves on to the next

22

step (rOper1+1) in our rule to see if it's a number. This is the first introduction to the power of "Ignore" in temporal logic.

	Rule	**State**	**True Action**	**Next**	**False Action**	**Next**
	rOper1	= <iNeg44>?	Negate		Ignore	
Time➔						

Table 4.0
COSA Extended BNF

If the "on-click" event in "rOper1" is a digit (Table 4.1), we add the digit to our integer portion of the number we are building and return control to the Windows Message Loop, and we remain at this step in time until we no longer receive a digit as an action. As long as a digit is entered, the logic remains at this temporal step and the true action "Any_Number" continues to build the integer portion of the number. After each digit is received the true action "Any_Number" turns off the calculator engine. When a non-digit button is clicked the logic at the digit step is false and executes the false "Ignore" behavior, transitioning to the next step in time looking for a period.

	Rule	**State**	**True Action**	**Next**	**False Action**	**Next**
	rOper1	= < iNeg44>?	Negate	rOper1+1	Ignore	rOper1+1
Time➔	+1	= <iDigit>*	Any_Number	rOper1+1	Ignore	rOper1+2

Table 4.1
COSA Extended BNF

If the "on-click" event is a period <iDot59> the number being built becomes a floating-point number (Table 4.2). The period is added to the number string and the calculator engine is turned off by the "One_Period" action. Time transitions to the fractional part of the number, and control is returned to the Windows Message Loop. Control remains with the "Any_Number" fractional part until a non-digit is entered.

23

Then the false "Ignore" behavior is executed, and control searches for the next step or rule.

Rule	State	True Action	Next	False Action	Next
rOper1	= <iNeg44>?	Negate		Ignore	
+1	= <iDigit>*	Any_Number		Ignore	
+2	= <iDot59>?	One_Period		Ignore	rOper1+4
+3	= <iDigit>*	Any_Number	rOper1+3	Ignore	rOper1+4
Time→	+4				

Table 4.2
COSA Extended BNF

If the entry isn't a decimal point, then the transition is to the "Clear Entry" step. If "CE" is clicked, then the display is cleared and the transition is back to the first step <iNeg44> otherwise the false "Ignore" behavior is executed and the next step, "Clear", is considered (Table 4.3). If "C" is clicked, the display is cleared and the transition is back to the first step <iNeg44>, otherwise the false "Ignore" behavior is executed, and time moves to the next temporal step of completing the first operand.

Rule	State	True Action	Next	False Action	Next
rOper1	= < iNeg44>?	Negate		Ignore	
+1	= <iDigit>*	Any_Number		Ignore	
+2	= <iDot59>?	One_Period	rOper1+3	Ignore	rOper1+4
+3	= <iDigit>*	Any_Number		Ignore	
+4	= <iClEnt>?	Clear_Entry	rOper1	Ignore	
+5	= <iClear>?;	Clear	rOper1	Ignore	rOper1+6
+6	= <iPush>	Push_Disp	rOper8	Push_Disp	rOper8
Time→					

Table 4.3
COSA Extended BNF

At this point, most of these Rule/Step transitions should be obvious. What isn't obvious to the customer is the internal housekeeping that needs to be undertaken. The customer doesn't recognize the need of moving and saving values for further actions. As the analyst, we know that we are going to operate on two values and therefore must keep those two values around somewhere through an appropriate state and action. In Table 4.3 the action "Push_Disp" is created to convert the first operand string to a number and save it for the anticipated calculation.

rOper8:

Now there is a number ready to operate on. Any match in "rOper8" moves time to "rOper2". For the sake of discussion, let's assume the operation "*" (multiply) was clicked. In Table 4.4, the calculator engine "Ignores" its way from the fractional portion of the first operand at step "rOper1+3", past "rOper8", and "rOper8+1", to "rOper8+2" the logic of <iMul42>. At this point the engine found a match between the dynamic state from the user's click and the static state in the rule. With a match at "rOper8+2" time moves to the next rule at "rOper2".

	Rule	State	True Action	Next	False Action	Next
	rOper1	= <iNeg44>?	Negate		Ignore	
	+1	= <iDigit>*	Any_Number		Ignore	
	+2	= <iDot59>?	One_Period		Ignore	
	+3	= <iDigit>*	Any_Number		Ignore	
	+4	= <iClEnt>?	Clear_Entry		Ignore	
	+5	= <iClear>?;	Clear		Ignore	
	+6	= <iPush>	Push_Disp		Push_Disp	
	rOper8	= <iAdd43>?	Addition		Ignore	rOper8+1
	+1	= <iSub44>?	Subtraction		Ignore	rOper8+2
Time→	+2	= <iMul42>?	Multiply	rOper2	Ignore	
	+3	= <iDiv47>?;	Division		Ignore	rError

Table 4.4
COSA Extended BNF

<u>rOper2:</u>

At this time the calculator engine has transitioned to the next rule, "rOper2", where any state, true or false, is allowed to turn off the engine. In each of the true actions, "Addition", "Subtraction", "Multiply", and "Division", a line of code could have been added to turn the engine off. In this example, the analyst chose to add a line of logic to indicate that the engine is explicitly turned off. With the action "Engine_Off", the temporal pointer has the calculator engine waiting for the next "on-click" event for the second operand to be entered.

	Rule	**State**	**True Action**	**Next**	**False Action**	**Next**
	rOper1	= \<iNeg44\>?	Negate		Ignore	
	+1	= iDigit\>*	Any_Number		Ignore	
	+2	= \<iDot59\>?	One_Period		Ignore	
	+3	= \<iDigit\>*	Any_Number		Ignore	
	+4	= \<iClEnt\>?	Clear_Entry		Ignore	
	+5	= \<iClear\>?;	Clear		Ignore	
	+6	= \<iPush\>	Push_Disp		Push_Disp	
	rOper8	= \<iAdd43\>?	Addition		Ignore	
	+1	= \<iSub44\>?	Subtraction		Ignore	
	+2	= \<iMul42\>?	Multiply		Ignore	
	+3	= \<iDiv47\>?;	Division		Ignore	
	rOper2	= \<iOff\>	Engine_Off	rOper2+1	Engine_Off	rOper2+1
Time→	+1					

Table 4.5
COSA Extended BNF

As we continue with "rOper2" the logic associated with the second operand is like the logic of first operand with the addition of the "Save_Disp" true or false behavior after the \<iClear\> step (Table 4.6). The "Save_Disp" action creates the second number ready for the appropriate operator action. When the second operand has been entered and "CE" or "C" haven't been clicked then the "rOper2" rule transitions control to the "rResult" rule.

26

Rule	State	True Action	Next	False Action	Next
rOper1	= \<iNeg44\>?	Negate		Ignore	
+1	= \<iDigit\>*	Any_Number		Ignore	
+2	= \<iDot59\>?	One_Period		Ignore	
+3	= \<iDigit\>*	Any_Number		Ignore	
+4	= \<iClEnt\>?	Clear_Entry		Ignore	
+5	= \<iClear\>?;	Clear		Ignore	
+6	= \<iPush\>	Push_Disp		Push_Disp	
rOper8	= \<iAdd43\>?	Addition		Ignore	
+1	= \<iSub44\>?	Subtraction		Ignore	
+2	= \<iMul42\>?	Multiply		Ignore	
+3	= \<iDiv47\>?;	Division		Ignore	
rOper2	= \<iOff\>	Engine_Off		Engine_Off	
+1	= \<iNeg44\>?	Negate		Ignore	
+2	= \<iDigit\>*	Any_Number		Ignore	
+3	= \<iDot59\>?	One_Period		Ignore	
+4	= \<iDigit\>*	Any_Number		Ignore	
+5	= \<iClEnt\>?	Clear_Entry	rOper2	Ignore	rOper2+6
+6	= \<iClear\>?;	Clear	rOper1	Ignore	rOper2+7
Time→ +7	= \<iSave\>	Save_Disp	rResult	Save_Disp	rResult

Table 4.6
COSA Extended BNF

rResult:

Time moves to the "rResult" rule from "rOper2" if the percent sign or the equal sign is clicked. The proper calculation is executed, the result is displayed, the temporal pointer is returned to the proper rule "rOper1", and the engine is turned off. Selecting the proper operation for the calculator isn't part of the actual mechanism of the control-flow logic. The actual mechanism is to setup a generic procedure pointer to execute the operation when the equal button is selected. As such, that mechanism doesn't show up in the logic table. The following table shows the complete rules for the calculator as specified by the customer.

	Rule	State	True Action	Next	False Action	Next
Time→	rOper1	= \<iNeg44\>?	Negate		Ignore	
	+1	= \<iDigit\>*	Any_Number		Ignore	
	+2	= \<iDot59\>?	One_Period		Ignore	
	+3	= \<iDigit\>*	Any_Number		Ignore	
	+4	= \<iClEnt\>?	Clear_Entry		Ignore	
	+5	= \<iClear\>?;	Clear		Ignore	
	+6	= \<iPush\>	Push_Disp		Push_Disp	
	rOper8	= \<iAdd43\>?	Addition		Ignore	
	+1	= \<iSub44\>?	Subtraction		Ignore	
	+2	= \<iMul42\>?	Multiply		Ignore	
	+3	= \<iDiv47\>?;	Division		Ignore	
	rOper2	= \<iOff\>	Engine_Off		Engine_Off	
	+1	= \<iNeg44\>?	Negate		Ignore	
	+2	= \<iDigit\>*	Any_Number		Ignore	
	+3	= \<iDot59\>?	One_Period		Ignore	
	+4	= \<iDigit\>*	Any_Number		Ignore	
	+5	= \<iClEnt\>?	Clear_Entry		Ignore	
	+6	= \<iClear\>?;	Clear		Ignore	
	+7	= \<iSave\>	Save_Disp		Save_Disp	
	rResult	= \<iPerc37\>	Percent	rOper1	Ignore	rResult+1
	+1	= \<iEqual\>	Equals	rOper1	Ignore	rResult+2
	+2	= \<iErr86\>	Error	rOper1	Error	rOper1

Table 4.7
COSA Extended BNF

The "rResult" rule completes the COSA logic for the calculator.   An error-handling step has been added to the "rResult" rule. This error-handling step will be connected to the false action of the \<iDiv47\> step in the "rOper8" rule. The next chapter on procedures provides the internal detail of the behaviors.

The COSA Extended BNF Rules Table

As a part of the ongoing review process the assigned trace numbers have stayed correlated with the customer's specification and the application's logic.   The process of correlating between the specification and the implementation can result in finding feature creep, i.e. things being added that were not requested, and specification completeness. This correlation process can also point out errors or weaknesses that may require additions to the specification.

The specification is repeated here to show how it correlates with the trace. The user enters a number (trace 100), the user enters an operator (trace 500), the user enters a second number (trace 700), and finally hits an equal key (trace 901) to get a result. Our user also asked to be able to correct entries (trace 104 and 705) or clear everything (trace 105 and 706).

Also our user wants to use the second operand to calculate a percent (trace 900) of the first operand. The user only understands simple numbers with decimal points (trace 101-103 & 701-703), and nothing else. The user decides the calculator needs additional functionality to be useful; a feature needs to be added. The ability to chain operations (trace 902) has been authorized as an addition to the specification.

The result is now defined in terms of being able to continue additional operations allowing the chaining together of operations as one would do in summing several numbers.

iChain = <rOper8> <rOper2>;

The <iChain> definition reuses the "rOper8" rule and the second operand "rOper2" to continue calculations. Table 4.8 shows the completed BNF as it was implemented with the temporal connections filled in from the reasoning process we have just gone through.

// // Rule	Static State	True Action	Next True Rule	False Action	Next False Rule	Trace
rOper1,	iNeg44,	Negate,	rOper1+1,	Ignore,	rOper1+1,	100
rOper1+1,	iDigit,	Any_Number,	rOper1+1,	Ignore,	rOper1+2,	101
rOper1+2,	iDot59,	One_Period,	rOper1+3,	Ignore,	rOper1+4,	102
rOper1+3,	iDigit,	Any_Number,	rOper1+3,	Ignore,	rOper1+4,	103
rOper1+4,	iClEnt,	Clear_Entry,	rOper1,	Ignore,	rOper1+5,	104
rOper1+5,	iClear,	Clear,	rOper1,	Ignore,	rOper1+6,	105
rOper1+6,	iPush,	Push_Disp,	rOper8,	Push_Disp,	rOper8,	106
// operate						
rOper8,	iAdd43,	Addition,	rOper2,	Ignore,	rOper8+1,	500
rOper8+1,	iSub44,	Subtraction,	rOper2,	Ignore,	rOper8+2,	501
rOper8+2,	iMul42,	Multiply,	rOper2,	Ignore,	rOper8+3,	502
rOper8+3,	iDiv47,	Division,	rOper2,	Ignore,	rError,	503
// next operand						
rOper2,	iOff,	Engine_Off,	rOper2+1,	Eng_Off,	rOper2+1,	700
rOper2+1,	iNeg44,	Negate,	rOper2+2,	Ignore,	rOper2+2,	701
rOper2+2,	iDigit,	Any_Number,	rOper2+2,	Ignore,	rOper2+3,	702
rOper2+3,	iDot59,	One_Period,	rOper2+4,	Ignore,	rOper2+5,	703
rOper2+4,	iDigit,	Any_Number,	rOper2+4,	Ignore,	rOper2+5,	704
rOper2+5,	iClEnt,	Clear_Entry,	rOper2+1,	Ignore,	rOper2+6,	705
rOper2+6,	iClear,	Clear,	rOper1,	Ignore,	rOper2+7,	706
rOper2+7,	iSave,	Save_Disp,	rResult,	Save_Disp,	rResult,	707
// equals						
rResult,	iPer37,	Percent,	rOper1,	Ignore,	rResult+1,	900
rResult+1,	iEqual,	Equals,	rOper1,	Ignore,	rResult+2,	901
rResult+2,	iChain,	Operate,	rOper8,	Operate,	rError,	902
rError,	iErr86,	Unknown,	rOper1,	Error,	rOper1,	993

Table 4.8
Completed COSA Extended BNF

The COSA extended BNF Rules Table uses columns to define:

1) The rule name and step
2) What is being looked for – static state
3) What to do with the item when it is found – true Action
4) What to do next after the item has been dealt with – next true rule
5) What to do if the item is not found – false Action
6) What to do next when the desired item is not found – next false rule
7) A trace of what has been done.

Furthermore, the Action columns are dynamically bound to the engine and represent *behaviors* while the individual cells in the Action columns represent the *methods* of the class. The "Negate" method is referred to as a behavior when it is executed from the engine.

Understanding COSA States

One definition of cohesion is, "Do one thing and do it well." Each row in the COSA Extended BNF Rules Table is a state; each state is a step in a rule. Each row does this one state very well. Each row provides for a true and a false behavior for the engine and a true and a false next step and trace.

Accurate documentation is an added benefit of the COSA Extended BNF Rules Table. The documentation can be shown as a spreadsheet or in tree format, expanded or collapsed. If management wants a verbal description, a narrative can to be attached as a link to each row.

In contrast to how COSA states are defined, in another example of a calculator,[23] Horrocks creates eight states to describe the five-function calculator. They are numbered and labeled as:

1) Start,
2) Negative Number,
3) Operand1,
4) Operator Entered,
5) Negative Number,
6) Operand2 and C,
7) Alert (message), and
8) Result.

[23] Horrocks, Ian, *Constructing the User Interface with Statecharts*, pp. 115-121, Addison-Wesley, 1999.

These eight states are low in cohesion because each state will do many things. In an attempt to explain a state authors and analysts add transitional narrative to the connection (transition) arrows between the states contributing further to a low level of cohesion (Figure 4.0).

Software developers will interpret the narrative in different ways causing many different results. A critic might argue that these state diagrams are meant to be abstract and not part of the implementation. Each transitive narrative in Figure 4.0 is devoid of any explicit time. Without a temporal component the developer must make decisions about the software design based on professional experience. And there is conflict in Figure 4.0 between what a transitive narrative (CE) does and what a state (C) does. Clear entry is defined as a transition while clear is defined as a state. In this situation the developer could choose to require a second operand be successfully entered before the clear can even be used.

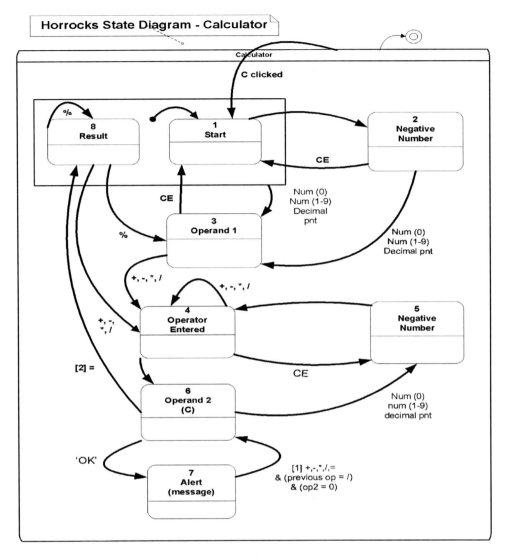

Figure 4.0
Another ITE Calculator Statechart

The logic of high abstraction is why the MDA approach continues to have problems. At some point in time (no pun intended), all of the information must be present under the abstraction for MDA to succeed. The generally accepted use of highly abstract statecharts will continue to contribute to MDA not meeting its full potential.

In a different example of how states are treated the CMU-SEI "L7 State Machines.ppt" presentation[24] shows mixing data manipulation and control-flow in the same diagram. Mixing reduces the cohesion of the design. The COSA Extended BNF Table doesn't support mixing of data manipulation because it can only represent logic.

The COSA Extended BNF Table 4.8 shown previously is a part of the model and it is the logic of the application. This makes it consistent with the state diagram because the state diagram is drawn from the BNF. The choice is to view the COSA Extended BNF Table or the Graphic Tree as in Tree 4.0 shown earlier created from the BNF. Changes to the BNF are reflected in the Graphic Tree, and changes to the Graphic Tree are reflected in the BNF. The model and application remain in sync and coherent.

All COSA states are binary and are managed by the temporal cursor iTime[25]. When a COSA state diagram is produced the states are numbered with their respective trace values. These states generally transition in chronological order. Transitioning to earlier states or repeating states forms iterative loops.

The engine definition and a couple of engine controls have been added to the BNF. The <iOff> control stops the engine and allows control to return to the Windows Message Loop. The definition of <iDigit> is that any single digit can be entered. Every time a digit is entered into the calculator the engine is turned off and control is returned to the Windows Message Loop to wait for the next event. This allows the calculator to build complex numbers one digit at a time.

---

[24] "Personal Software Process/Team Software Process" slide 19, Sponsored by U.S. Department of Defense – © 2005 by CMU.
[25] So that the rules will fit on a single line portrait orientation, programmer-abbreviated names like "rOper8" and <iNeg44> are used.

The <iPush> and <iSave> are the display values being used in the calculation. The <iPush> state keeps the first value available to be used in the subsequent operation calculation. The <iSave> state is specific to the potential to chain operations.

The state diagram in Figure 4.1 doesn't need narrative labels to describe transitions to other states. Because of the high level of cohesion, each state has only true or false transitions. There is little room for errors in interpretation with a COSA binary state diagram.

The solid lines represent true logic and dashed lines represent the false logic (when it doesn't matter if the result is true or false that logic is represented by a dash-dot line). The model is the application whether the model is represented as BNF, tree diagram, state diagram, or UML boxes-with-strings; the consistency is easy to keep.

The COSA State Diagram (Figure 4.1) is easy to understand. The inner box labeled "Oper1" contains the states that build the first operand. The inner box labeled "Oper8" contains the operators add, subtract, multiply, and divide. The inner box labeled "Oper2" contains the states that build the second operand. And the inner box labeled "Result" performs the work related to the selected operation. Anyone that can use a five-function calculator should be able to understand the flow of logic in the statechart in figure 4.1.

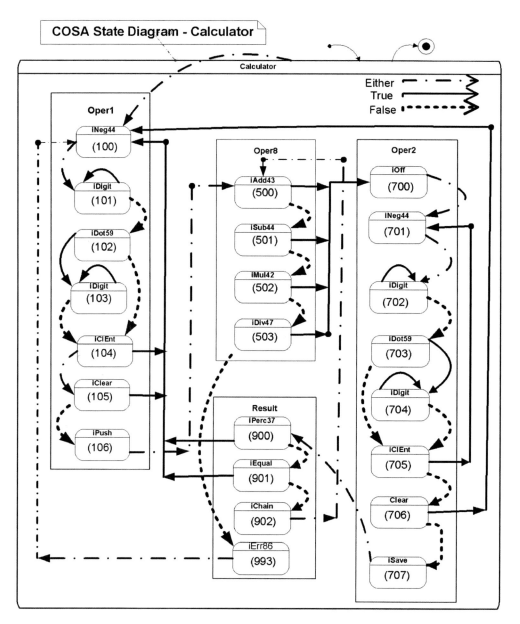

Figure 4.1
COSA State Diagram

Notice how the following domain-specific BNF 4.1 is still synchronized with the state diagram of Figure 4.1. The state diagram of Figure 4.1 is just a different representation of the COSA Extended BNF Rules Table 4.8.

Engine	= <Calculate>;
Calculate	= <rOper1> <rOper8> <rOper2> <rResult>?;
rOper1 (100)	= <iNeg44>? <iDigit>* (<iDot59> <iDigit>+)? (<iClEnt>? | <iClear>?) <iPush>;
iDigit	= (<0> | <1> | <2> | <3> | <4> | <5> | <6> | <7> | <8> | <9>)+;
rOper8 (500)	= <iAdd43> | <iSub44> | <iMul42> | <iDiv47>;
rOper2 (700)	= <iOff> (<iNeg44>? <iDigit>* (<iDot59> <iDigit>+)?) (<iClEnt>? | <iClear>?) <iSave>;
rResult (900)	= (<iPerc> | <iEquals> | <iChain>);
iChain	= <rOper8> <rOper2>
iClrEnt	= Clear the current display and value
iClear	= <iClrEnt> & restart
iOff	= Turn local engine control off
iPush	= Save the current displayed value
iSave	= Save the last calculation result

BNF 4.1
COSA Calculator

The rules are shown as dominate (left justified) in the column under Engine. In addition to starting with the lower case "r", the rules make up the reference point for events in time. The steps/states start with the lower case "i" and become the steps within their respective rules.

Operational Analysis of the COSA Rules Table

The operational analysis provides a runtime understanding of the logic. The operation and the initial test of the calculator are divided into four parts:

1)   Operand one is "–3.14159",
2)   The operation is "–",

3)   Operand two is "–2.14159", and

4)   "=" Produces a result of "–1".

Using the mouse to click on the calculator-form enters each digit or decimal point into the display. Clicking on an operator will result in the display being cleared for the next operand to be entered. The trace files from both COSA and ITE approach will show the state transitions. The complete individual trace files for both applications are attached as appendices A and B.

The calculator starts in the "Run" state at trace 100 (t100). This simple calculator does not have a change sign button, so clicking on the "-" sign to negate a number can only happen before a number is entered as the first operand. Step 1) of the test starts with clicking on the minus sign to create a negative number. This is the <iNeg44> state at t100.

For more detail, the "expanded" COSA state diagram in Appendix I shows the state name, e.g. <iNeg44>, the true behavior "Negate," and the false behavior "Ignore," a true next state solid arrow, and a false next state dashed arrow. (If at this time these details aren't import to you, continue to refer to Figure 4.1.)

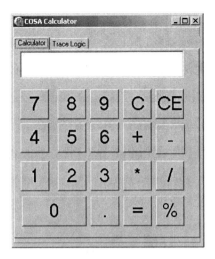

Figure 4.2
COSA Calculator Form

Logically it doesn't matter whether the first entity is a negative sign or not. The next "iTime" transition will be the whole portion of the number being built. The temporal component keeps track of its time sequence in the operational loop eliminating the need for any ambiguous group of flags or variables. Whether the state is true or false, there is only one temporal target for leaving the <iNeg44> state: the <iDigit> state t101.

Continuing our test, the number 3 button is clicked, and the next "iTime" remains at <iDigit> state at t101. Figure 4.0 shows the <iDigit> state at t101 repeating, this happens until the button clicked on the calculator is not a number.

The period button is clicked, and "iTime" transitions to the <iDot59> state at t102. Like the <iNeg44> state at t100, the <iDot59> state at t102 can only transition to the next state, <iDigit> state t103. Since only one period is allowed in a valid number, the transition must be to another "iTime". As the fractional portion of the number is entered, "14159", the "iTime" iterates on the <iDigit> state at t103 until the button clicked is not a number.

Step 2) An operation button is clicked, the subtract in this example, and "iTime" transitions through <iClEnt> state at t104 as false, through <iClear> state at t105 as false, through <iPush> state at t106 as false, through the <iAdd43> state at t500 as false, and finally to the <iSub44> subtraction state at t501 as true. The true operation rule sends the next "iTime" to <iOff> at t700 skipping the other operator states at t502 and t503. State <iOff> turns the engine off sending control back to the Windows Message Loop to wait for the next button click.

After an operation has been entered and before the second operand is entered, the unary minus can be entered for the second operand. The trace files, in Appendix A & B, compare COSA at step 17 to the ITE approach at a range from step 55 to step 61.

Step 3) The operation and second operand look like this "- - 2.14159" with back-to-back button clicks on the negative, one for the operation and one for the unary minus. "iTime" transitions to <iNeg44> state at t701, followed by <iDigit> state at t702, then the <iDot59> state at t703, and finally the <iDigit> state at t704. The temporal connections are similar to the first operand. The behaviors are the same since the first operand was pushed internally using "Push_Disp" for the calculation coming up.

Step 4) At this stage the equal sign "=" is clicked to create a result. "iTime" transitions to <iClEnt> state at t705 as false, <iClear> state at t706 as false, then to <iSave> state at t707 as false. The next state checked is <iPerc37> state at t900 as false, then to <iEqual> state at t901 as true, producing the result.

Seventeen state events were entered for this calculation example. Doing the same calculation the complete COSA trace shows 30 state transitions (Appendix A), as compared to the 95 state transitions in the complete ITE trace (Appendix B). More than

3.1 times the number of states must be transitioned in order to do the work using traditional "if-then-else" logic.

The ITE State Diagram View

The contents of the COSA Extended BNF Table can clearly be seen in the COSA state diagram in Figure 4.1. Since each row in the COSA Extended BNF Table 4.8 has two possible state transitions and, as would be expected, the state diagram also has two possible transitions to the next state: true or false. The predictability of this binary state design greatly simplifies the transition logic compared to the multiple state transitions in the ITE traditional approach shown in Figure 4.3.

The ITE statechart shows three transitions out of the "ready" (1) state, four transitions from the "negated1" (3) state, and five transitions into the "opEntered" (8) state. The temporal component is missing in the state diagram of Figure 4.3. Comparing the trace files for the two applications the simplification produced by COSA can be seen. When both applications enter "-3.14159" the progress is at count number 9 in the COSA trace file (Appendix A), as compared to count number 47 in the ITE trace file (Appendix B).

There has been a significant amount written[26] about the extremely difficult task of verifying software. The reduction in complexity along with the increased trace coverage provided by a COSA implementation can make this "Grand Challenge" quite manageable when compared to ITE.

The following statement about the ITE State Diagram in Figure 4.3 makes it clear why we have so many problems with software correctness and verification. As Samek

---

[26] "First Steps in the Verified Software Grand Challenge", *IEEE Computer Society*, Jim Woodcock, October 2006

points out: "Arriving at this statechart was definitely not trivial, and you shouldn't worry if you don't fully understand it at the first reading (I wouldn't either)."[27]

Not only is this statechart in Figure 4.3 "not trivial to understand", it is equally not trivial to program and any software engineer should worry about its implementation.

---

[27] Samek, Miro, PhD, *Practical Statecharts in C/C++,* page 8, section 1.2.2, CPM Books © 2002.

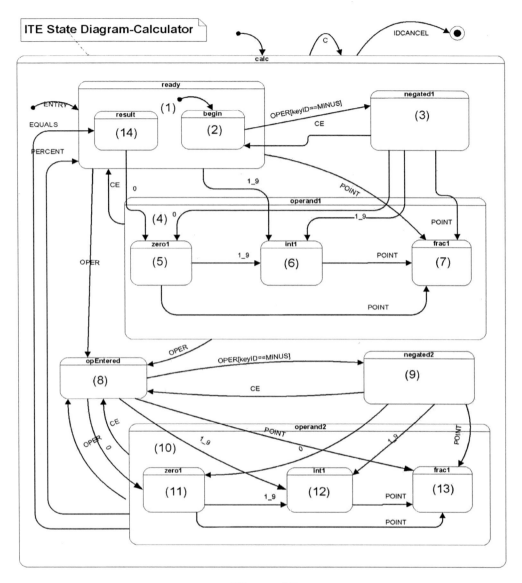

Figure 4.3
ITE Calculator Statechart

Statecharts should make understanding the solution easier, and they should be highly cohesive defining one state and doing it very well. This rule should never be broken.

43

Summary

This chapter covered the correlation of the specification with the BNF, which then led to the creation of a tree that then produced the COSA Extended BNF Table. Each of these steps represents different refined views of the same information.

In the process of building the COSA Extended BNF Table the static states represent what is expected at each step in time. This approach results in a very simple and easy to understand statechart that is unambiguous because each step in time can only produce a true or false result.

In the traditional ITE approach without an understanding of time, flags *must* be set throughout the application to indicate in which mode the application is at any given time. The ITE state machine approach results in a very complex statechart[28]. Designers, modelers, and authors put forth statecharts with labeled arrows between states. These labeled arrows create an ambiguous meaning because they are open to interpretation.

---

[28] Samek, Miro, *Practical Statecharts in C/C++*, 2002 CMP Books, page 8.

5

Chapter 5 – The COSA Engine in Detail

COSA uses three structures to develop the objects that make up an application: engine, control-flow table, and data-flow methods. The engine is a single point of control that time-manages the running of an object. The control-flow table contains the rules associated with the object and determines the object's runtime logical behavior. The data-flow methods (procedures) use no arguments since they should only be called from within the object controlled by the engine and the control-flow table. The only entry into the object should be through the engine and the interfaces it defines. This makes for a very nice "black-box" software chip design.

```
1  procedure TCOSAcalc.Run(intState : integer; sNumber : String);
2  begin
3        engLocal := TRUE;
4        dynamicState := intState;
5        sArgValue := sNumber;
6        while (engLocal) AND (engGlobal) do
7        begin
8              if dynamicState = rRule[iTime].staticState then
9              begin
10                   rRule[iTime].pTrueRule;           // Dynamically True Behavior
11                   True_Trace(iTime);                // TRUE TRACE GREEN
12                   iTime := rRule[iTime].iTrueRule;  // Next True Rule Time
13             end else
14             begin
15                   rRule[iTime].pFalseRule;          // Dynamically False Behavior
16                   False_Trace(iTime);               // FALSE TRACE RED
17                   iTime := rRule[iTime].iFalseRule;  // Next False Rule Time
18             end;
19       formCalc.editdisplay.Text := sBuildNumber;
20 end;
```

Code Segment 5.0
Delphi COSA Calculator Engine

The engine is preempted by a false condition on line 6, with the engine's "while" statement. The local control and global control are designed into the overall application to handle its runtime execution. If either the global control or local control are false, the engine will cease execution. No matter how many objects have been instantiated below a COSA object, they can be terminated quickly with the global control, provided that a procedure does not contain an infinite loop.

The importance of the "while" statement cannot be overstated; it provides the single point of control and the ability to preempt after each iteration of the instantiated object. An application's designer should always take this fact into consideration. Behaviors that are complex and take a long time to return control to the engine circumvent this important architectural feature.

In the calculator example the local engine state "engLocal" is the control for running the engine within the object. The engine state "engGlobal" allows for global control to terminate the object separately from the local control. Monitoring the global engine state, with a high priority thread, can control graceful and emergency shutdowns. Other engine states can be joined in conjunction for control scenarios that are beyond this introduction.

The trace mechanism is built into the engine as an inherent part of COSA. Trace covers 100% of the logic because it is centralized in the engine. There can be two trace methods, one for the true behavior and one for the false behavior. Using two different trace methods allows for differing levels of detail on the true and false behaviors. Alternatively, there can be a single trace where the argument is signed to indicate true or false behaviors. Either way, trace can be as robust as desired to cover the logic and data manipulation. The procedure calls to the trace routines are at lines 11 and 16 in this Delphi implementation of the COSA engine.

Centralized Control of Runtime

The dynamic state is passed into the engine by the object's interface and is passed to the "if" statement of line 8. This is the only "if" statement in each COSA Engine. The origin of the dynamic state for this application is from the "on-click" message logic of Windows. The "if" compares the dynamic state to the static state of the current (iTime) temporal rule or step within the control-flow logic.

The dynamic binding statements at lines 10 and 15 are very technically complex. The COSA dynamic binding statements provide a consistent way to include both "Polymorphism and Dynamic Binding" into an engineered[29] approach.

Polymorphism and Dynamic Binding

"Polymorphism and dynamic binding offer a first step to developing software that runs in an open world. As an example, suppose that an application is initially designed to deal with a certain device, such as a fax machine. Through a variable f of class Fax, you can send a fax by writing f.sendFax(t,n), where t is a text and n is a fax number.

Suppose that you later add to the system a new device, such as a fax with phone, which provides its own way of sending faxes. If FaxWithPhone is a derived class of Fax, which redefines operation sendFax, variable f can refer to it, and the result of f.sendFax(t,n) would result in sending the fax using the redefined method of class FaxWithPhone. More important, the client component that uses variable f to send faxes isn't affected by the change.

The compiler checks for correctness by assuming that f's type is defined by class Fax, but the invocation of sendFax is ensured to be correct even if the dynamic type of the object referred by f is FaxWithPhone. Indeed, the client continues to work correctly with the newly defined device as it did earlier.

This simple example shows that the flexibility that polymorphism and dynamic binding provide can coexist with the discipline and safety that strong typing supports." [30]

---

[29] Samek, Milo PhD, "Dynamic binding in C++," page 74 (this→*myState)(e).
[30] "Agile Programming: Design to Accommodate" – *IEEE Software* May/June 2005 – Dave Thomas.

What Thomas is referring to in his *IEEE* article is replacing an old object (Fax) with a new object (FaxWithPhone) and the new device works just like the old one. But what about the new features provided by the new device? Polymorphism alone does not allow new features to be dynamically bound with the new device without replacing the parent or calling object. COSA provides more than polymorphism. The combination of the COSA engine and the COSA Extended BNF Table provide an environment where the table can be used to *learn* new behaviors by dynamically changing the rules. The parent object that called the old object (Fax) and the new object (FaxWithPhone) can have new rules added to handle the new features. Suppose that the FaxWithPhone new feature is to redial "n" times when a busy line is detected. The parent object doesn't know about the new feature. If the parent object is a COSA object, then the parent's rules can be changed to allow for the new feature.

In this example the COSA Extended BNF Table (Table 5.0), the columns called "True Actions" and "False Actions" are dynamically bound methods in this example. When the dynamic state is the same as the static state in line 8 of the engine, then the true behavior is dynamically bound[31] and executed at line 10. When control is returned to the engine, the trace at line 11 is called, followed by line 12, setting the temporal location for the next rule to be executed.

When the dynamic state is NOT the same as the static state in line 8 of the engine then the FALSE behavior is dynamically bound and executed at line 15. When control is returned to the engine, the FALSE trace at line 16 is called, followed by line 17, setting the temporal location for the next rule to be executed.

---

[31] Toward Open-World Software: Issues and Challenges – IEEE Computer Society – October 2006 – Luciano Baresi, Elisabetta Di Nitto, and Carlo Ghezzi.

48

For example, if the first button clicked is a number then the dynamic state is not "iNeg44" and the engine will execute the false behavior "Ignore" at rule "rOper1" and transition to the next step using the entry in the Next False Rule column.

//
//Rule
//Step
	Static
	State
		True
		Actions
			Next
			True
			Rule
				False
				Actions
					Next
					False
					Rule
						Trace

// Operand 1						
rOper1,	iNeg44,	Negate,	rOper1+1,	Ignore,	rOper1+1,	100
rOper1+1,	iDigit,	Any_Number,	rOper1+1,	Ignore,	rOper1+2,	101
rOper1+2,	iDot59,	One_Period,	rOper1+3,	Ignore,	rOper1+4,	102
rOper1+3,	iDigit,	Any_Number,	rOper1+3,	Ignore,	rOper1+4,	103
rOper1+4,	iClEnt,	ClearEntry,	rOper1,	Ignore,	rOper1+5,	104
rOper1+5,	iClear,	Clear,	rOper1,	Ignore,	rOper1+6,	105
rOper1+6,	iPush,	Push_Disp,	rOper8,	Push_Disp	rOper8,	106
// Operator						
rOper8,	iAdd43	Addition,	rOper2,	Ignore,	rOper8+1,	500
rOper8+1,	iSub44	Subtraction	rOper2,	Ignore,	rOper8+2,	501
rOper8+2,	iMul42	Multiply,	rOper2,	Ignore,	rOper8+3,	502
rOper8+3,	iDiv47	Division,	rOper2,	Ignore,	rError,	503
// Operand 2						
rOper2,	iOff,	Engine_Off,	rOper2+1,	Eng_Off,	rOper2+1,	700
rOper2+1,	iNeg44,	Negate,	rOper2+2,	Ignore,	rOper2+2,	701
rOper2+2,	iDigit,	Any_Number,	rOper2+2,	Ignore,	rOper2+3,	702
rOper2+3,	iDot59,	One_Period,	rOper2+4,	Ignore,	rOper2+5,	703
rOper2+4,	iDigit,	Any_Number,	rOper2+4,	Ignore,	rOper2+5,	704
rOper2+5,	iClEnt,	ClearEntry,	rOper2+1,	Ignore,	rOper2+6,	705
rOper2+6,	iClear,	Clear,	rOper1,	Ignore,	rOper2+7,	706
rOper2+7,	iSave,	Save_Disp,	rResult,	Save_Disp	rResult,	707
// Result						
rResult,	iPer37,	Percent,	rOper1,	Ignore,	rResult+1,	900
rResult+1,	iEqual,	Equals,	rOper1,	Ignore,	rResult+2,	901
rResult+2,	iChain,	Operate,	rOper8,	Operate,	rOper8,	902
rError,	iErr86,	Unknown,	rOper1,	Error,	rOper1,	993

Table 5.0
COSA Extended BNF Rules

The COSA Engine Implementation in C++

The segment of code below is the calculator engine implemented in Microsoft C++. The essence of the structure is nearly identical compared to the Borland/Delphi approach.

The major difference is the pseudo object approach Microsoft uses in its implementation of the foundation class to access the calculator form objects. That is, Microsoft uses an IDC_EDIT1 value to look up the address of the calculator display object, "pEditWnd = GetDlgItem(IDC_EDIT1)," the result can be placed in the display object at line 17 below. Whereas, Borland/Delphi uses a true object path "formCalc.editdisplay.Text := sBuildNumber;" to place the result in the display object.

```
//************** C++ Implementation **********************
1  void aCalc::Run(int iState, LPCTSTR sDisplay) {
2      sNumber = sDisplay;
3      engCalc = 1;
4      dynamicState = iState;
5      while(engCalculate && engCalc){      //Local/Global preemption
6        if(dynamicState == Tbl[iTime].state)
7        {
8                COSA_Trace(iTime);               // 32
9                (this→*(Tbl[iTime].True_Behavior))();
10               iTime = Tbl[iTime].Next_True;
11       } else {
12               COSA_Trace(-iTime);
13               (this→*(Tbl[iTime].False_Behavior))();
14               iTime = Tbl[iTime].Next_False;
15       }
16     }
17     pEditWn→SetWindowText(_T(sBuildNumber)); // display
18 }

//*************** C++ Implementation **********************
```

Code Segment 5.1
C++ COSA Calculator Engine

---

[32] NOTE: There are times when the trace function call could be placed before the behaviors in the engine, as is the case in the C++ implementation.

The COSA Rules Table Implementation in C++

This implementation of the logic table in C++ is a little ugly.   The ugliness is created by the fully qualified path to the action that is required by the language (Version 6.0 Developer Studio). Since Delphi does not require this extra work, I have not experimented with ways around this fully qualified requirement.

```
//******************************** C++ Implementation ************************
// Calculator Table
struct aCalc::aCalc_Tbl Tbl[] = {       // statically build rules in table
//                        Next                        Next
//                        True          True          False         False
//  Rule       State      Behavior      Rule          Behavior      Rule      Trace
{ca(rOpr1,     iNeg44,    &aCalc::Negate,      rOpr1+1, &aCalc::Ignore,      rOpr1+1, 100)},
{ca(rOpr1+1,   iAny,      &aCalc::AnyNumber,   rOpr1+1, &aCalc::Ignore,      rOpr1+2, 101)},
{ca(rOpr1+2,   iDot59,    &aCalc::OnePeriod,   rOpr1+3, &aCalc::Ignore,      rOpr1+4, 102)},
{ca(rOpr1+3,   iAny,      &aCalc::AnyNumber,   rOpr1+3, &aCalc::Ignore,      rOpr1+4, 103)},
{ca(rOpr1+4,   iClEnt,    &aCalc::ClearEntry,  rOpr1,   &aCalc::Ignore,      rOpr1+5, 104)},
{ca(rOpr1+5,   iClear,    &aCalc::Clear,       rOpr1,   &aCalc::Ignore,      rOpr1+6, 105)},
{ca(rOpr1+6,   iAny,      &aCalc::PushDisp,    rOpr1,   &aCalc::PushDisp,    rOpr8,   106)},
// operations
{ca(rOpr8,     iAdd43,    &aCalc::Addition,    rOpr2,   &aCalc::Ignore,      rOpr8+1, 500)},
{ca(rOpr8+1,   iSub44,    &aCalc::Subtract,    rOpr2,   &aCalc::Ignore,      rOpr8+2, 501)},
{ca(rOpr8+2,   iMul42,    &aCalc::Multiply,    rOpr2,   &aCalc::Ignore,      rOpr8+3, 502)},
{ca(rOpr8+3,   iDiv47,    &aCalc::Division,    rOpr2,   &aCalc::Ignore,      rOpr2,   503)},
// next number
{ca(rOpr2,     iAny,      &aCalc::EngOff,      rOpr2+1, &aCalc::EngOff,      rOpr2+1, 700)},
{ca(rOpr2+1,   iNeg44,    &aCalc::Negate,      rOpr2+2, &aCalc::Ignore,      rOpr2+2, 701)},
{ca(rOpr2+2,   iAny,      &aCalc::AnyNumber,   rOpr2+2, &aCalc::Ignore,      rOpr2+3, 702)},
{ca(rOpr2+3,   iDot59,    &aCalc::OnePeriod,   rOpr2+4, &aCalc::Ignore,      rOpr2+5, 703)},
{ca(rOpr2+4,   iAny,      &aCalc::AnyNumber,   rOpr2+4, &aCalc::Ignore,      rOpr2+5, 704)},
{ca(rOpr2+5,   iAny,      &aCalc::SavDsp,      rOpr2+6, &aCalc::SavDsp,      rOpr2+6, 705)},
// clear
{ca(rOpr2+6,   iClEnt,    &aCalc::ClrEntr,     rOpr2+1, &aCalc::Ignore,      rOpr2+7, 706)},
{ca(rOpr2+7,   iClear,    &aCalc::Clear,       rOpr1,   &aCalc::Ignore,      rResu,   707)},
// equals
{ca(rResu,     iPer37,    &aCalc::Percent,     rOpr1,   &aCalc::Ignore,      rResu+1, 900)},
{ca(rResu+1,   iEqual,    &aCalc::Equals,      rOpr1,   &aCalc::Ignore,      rResu+2, 901)},
{ca(rResu+2,   iAny,      &aCalc::Operate,     rOpr8,   &aCalc::Operate,     rOpr8,   902)},
{ca(rErr,      iErr86,    &aCalc::Unknown,     rOpr1,   &aCalc::Error,       rOpr1,   993)}
};  // end of static build
//******************************** C++ Implementation **********************
```

Table 5.1
C++ COSA Extended BNF

The rules are initialized differently in a C++ implementation. There is a macro that defines the structure, and the rules are created statically. The macro allows the pre-compiler to properly create the structure. Notice the ending comma; it is critical to making the macro work correctly. Also, notice the comma at the end of each line in the C++ rules above and the last rule does not have a comma. Depending on the strength of the compiler, these can be difficult to find if they are omitted. (There are similar issues when it comes to implementing this in Java.)

```
#define rules(r,s,t,nt,f,nf,t) r,s,t,nt,f,nt,t,
```

In a multi-engine implementation in COSA, each engine has a control-flow table that contains the rules and their associated steps. The table in the calculator example uses seven columns. The seven columns are an indication of the structure of the engine. One column is used for the rule, and one column is used for the state. Two are used for true/false behaviors and two others are used for true/false transitions. The seventh and last column contains the trace value; in a large application this trace value could be something as large as a GUID[33].

In this particular implementation of the engine, the trace function is *"before"* the *"behaviors"* at lines 8 and 12. The rule is recorded in the object's trace mechanism before the step's operation has been performed.

Adding the Subordinate Percent Engine

The "Percent" operation only allows a sales tax type of calculation, i.e. value plus tax.

$$\$1.08 = \$1.00 \text{ plus } \$1.00 * (8\%)$$

---

[33] http://en.wikipedia.org/wiki/Globally_Unique_Identifier

In the ITE version of the calculator, the operations add, subtract, multiply, and divide are all allowed with percent. It's easy to add logic to an object by including a subordinate engine with rules and methods. In the initial design the "rResult" rule calls the proper operation through the dynamic bind variable. To perform the same functional flexibility, a subordinate engine and logical BNF are added to the original logic.

Every aspect of COSA can be viewed in a tree format. Because the percent procedures are relatively simple an interesting a new structure is introduced to the COSA Extended BNF Tree to define the actions of the data-flow procedures. Every section in COSA is labeled to keep them separate. Behind the scenes these structures are defined in XML and carry the necessary information to be complete.

{Control-Flow}	
Engine	= \<Calculate>\<rPerc>;
rPerc	= \<number > \<*>
	(\<iP_Add> | \<iP_Sub> | \<iP_Mul> | \<iPDiv>);
iP_Add	= \<pPerc_Add>;
iP_Sub	= \<pPerc_Sub>;
iP_Mul	= \<pPerc_Mul>;
iP_Div	= \<pPerc_Mul>;
{End Control-Flow}	
{Data-Flow}	
pPerc_Add	= (\<1> \<+> \<number>\</>\<100>); \<engPerc_Off>;
pPerc_Sub	= (\<1> \<-> \<number>\</>\<100>); \<engPerc_Off>;
pPerc_Mul	= \<number>\</>\<100>;\<engPerc_Off>;
pPerc_Div	= \<pPerc_Mul>;\<engPerc_Off>;
{End Data-Flow}	

Tree 5.0
COSA Percent Engine

When the percent button is clicked it calls on the new subordinate engine's logic to determine what operation was entered prior to the percent key being entered. The BNF remains consistent with the application.

```
Procedure TCOSAcalc.Percent();
begin
  while (engPerc) AND (engGlobal) do
  begin
        if pOperArg00 = rPercent[iTime].pOperState then
        begin
                rPercent[iTime].pTrueRule;          // Dynamically True Behavior
                True_Trace(iTime);                  // TRUE TRACE SOLID
                iTime := rPercent[iTime].iTrueRule; // Next True Rule Time
        end else
        begin
                rPercent[iTime].pFalseRule;          // Dynamically False Behavior
                False_Trace(iTime);                  // FALSE TRACE DASHED
                iTime := rPercent[iTime].iFalseRule; // Next False Rule Time
        end;
  sBuildNumber := FloatToStr(fNumber);
  bEngine := FALSE;                                  // Turn Main Engine Off
  end;
```

Code Segment 5.2
Delphi COSA Percent Engine

The logic in the percent engine is simple. If the operation is percent-addition then the dynamic token created will match the static state "iP_Add". The calculation is completed in the procedure "pPerc_Add" shown below which also turns off the percent engine. The two other percent calculations perform their same respective actions. The next false action on each rule is to skip-chain through the logic looking for a dynamic-static state match.

In the event that a match is not found then the final false action it to call the error routine.

Rule	Static State	True Action	Next True Rule	False Action	Next False Rule	Trace
rPerc,	iP_Add,	pPerc_Add,	rPerc+1,	Ignore,	rPerc+1,	1100
rPerc+1,	iP_Sub,	pPerc_Sub,	rPerc+1,	Ignore,	rPerc+2,	1101
rPerc+2,	iP_Mul,	pPerc_Mul,	rPerc+3,	Ignore,	rPerc+3,	1102
rPerc+3,	iP_Div,	pPerc_Mul,	rPerc+3,	Error,	rPerc+3,	1103

Table 5.2
Percent Extended BNF Rules

Listed here are the new procedures that are required to support a more robust percent type calculation:

```
Procedure TCOSAcalc.pPerc_Add();
begin
   fNumber := fNumber * (1.0 + fDisplay/100.0);
   engPerc := FALSE;
end;


procedure TCOSAcalc.pPerc_Sub();
begin
   fNumber := fNumber * (1.0 - fDisplay/100.0);
   engPerc := FALSE;
end;


procedure TCOSAcalc.pPerc_Mul();
begin
   fNumber := fNumber * fDisplay/100.0;
   engPerc := FALSE;
end;
```

Code Segment 5.3
Percent Calculation

The Final BNF Definition

There are two engines that run in the application now, the principle calculator engine, and whenever a percent operation is requested, the percent engine is engaged.

Engines	= <Calculate><Percent>;
Engine	= <Calculate>;
Calculate	= <rOper1> <rOper8> <rOper2> <rResult>?;
rOper1 (100)	= <iNeg44>? <iDigit>*(<iDot59><iDigit>+)? (<iClEnt>? | <iClear>?) <iPush> ;
iDigit	= (<0>|<1>|<2>|<3>|<4>|<5>|<6>|<7>|<8>|<9>)*;
rOper8 (500)	= <iAdd43>	<iSub44>	<iMul42>	<iDiv47>;
rOper2 (700)	= <Oper1> <iSave>;
rResult (900)	= <iOff> (<iPerc37> | <iEqual> | <iChain>);
iChain	= <rOper8>
iClrEnt	= Clear the current display and value
iClear	= <iClrEnt> & restart
iOff	= Turn local engine control off
iPush	= Save the current displayed value
iSave	= Save the last calculation result
Engine	= <Percent>;
Percent	= <rPerc>;
rPerc (1100)	= <number> <*> (<iP_Add > | <iP_Sub> | <iP_Mul> | <iPDiv>);

Tree 5.1
Final COSA Extended BNF

The final Tree 5.1 doesn't show the control-flow section so the focus is kept on the BNF structure of the logic.

Summary

The COSA engine implementation is consistent across languages. The COSA engine is truly a software component that can be used ubiquitously across the spectrum of applications. It can also be implemented as a subordinate engine expanding the logic of an object or procedural implementation.

The flexibility offered by the COSA engine also includes the ability to dynamically turn the engine's trace on and off by replacing the trace procedure call with dynamic binding to a trace method or an "ignore" method.

6

Chapter 6 – The COSA Methods in Detail

Chapter 6 covers what is left of traditional code development when the COSA engine and table have been implemented in a modeling tool. The part that remains to be manually coded is manipulation of the data. In domain-specific examples this can be as simple as drag and drop within a modeling tool. In an accounting application this is the formula, in an engineering application this is the equation. Each procedure or function is synchronized with a class definition and the control-flow defined by the COSA extended BNF.

The Methods in the GUI Class

There are two sections in the data-flow of this application: the GUI and the Logic. The GUI interfaces through the TformCalc Class. This class contains the "on-click" methods that are controlled by the Windows Message Loop as the buttons' event handlers. These "on-click" event handlers, like the multiply button event, are the access points to the COSA engine as shown in the following code segments. The "OnActivate" action is used to create the logic associated with the calculator form. This dynamic creation of the rules shown here is different from the C++ static approach.

```
Procedure TformCalc.CreateCOSA_OnActivate(Sender: Tobject);
begin
  objCOSA := TCOSAcalc.Create;
  objCOSA.CreateRules();       // create rules at runtime
end;
```

The Delphi GUI development environment creates the following procedures when the "on-click" event property is chosen. Each name is then edited to relate to the various buttons. It would have been nice to have one single "on-click" event that provided access to the text captions the buttons displayed, then a one button handler could have passed the text as the parser token for the BNF logic tree, but the "Sender: Tobject" didn't provide access to the button text.

```
Procedure TformCalc.SelectZero_OnClick(Sender: Tobject);
begin
  objCOSA.Run(1,'0');
end;

procedure TformCalc.SelectOne_OnClick(Sender: Tobject);
begin
  objCOSA.Run(1,'1');
end;

procedure TformCalc.SelectTwo_OnClick(Sender: Tobject);
begin
  objCOSA.Run(1,'2');
end;

procedure TformCalc.SelectThree_OnClick(Sender: Tobject);
begin
  objCOSA.Run(1,'3');
end;
```

The following "on-click" events are for the non-numbers. A numeric code was used for token values and the ASCII value where possible, like 43 decimal for the plus sign, to indicate the token's actual value when comparing the expected state to the dynamic state.

```
Procedure TformCalc.SelectClear_OnClick(Sender: Tobject);
begin
  objCOSA.Run(11,'');
end;


procedure TformCalc.SelectClearEntry_OnClick(Sender: Tobject);
```

```
begin
  objCOSA.Run(12,'');
end;

procedure TformCalc.SelectAddition_OnClick(Sender: Tobject);
begin
 objCOSA.run(43,'');
end;
procedure TformCalc.SelectSubtraction_OnClick(Sender:
Tobject);
begin
  objCOSA.run(44,'');
end;

procedure TformCalc.SelectMultiply_OnClick(Sender: Tobject);
begin
  objCOSA.run(42,'');
end;

procedure TformCalc.SelectDivide_OnClick(Sender: Tobject);
begin
  objCOSA.run(47,'');
end;

procedure TformCalc.SelectEquals_OnClick(Sender: Tobject);
begin
  objCOSA.run(13,'');
end;

procedure TformCalc.SelectPercent_OnClick(Sender: Tobject);
begin
  objCOSA.run(37,'');
end;
```

For the period "on-click" event the ASCII character gets passed to the engine and is used to build the number string. When the number string gets converted to a floating-point number the period is an essential part of the conversion.

```
Procedure TformCalc.SelectPeriod_OnClick(Sender: Tobject);
begin
  objCOSA.run(59,'.');
end;
```

The following method is simply used to clean up and release memory space after the application is done and shutting down.

60

```
Procedure TformCalc.CloseTraceFile_OnClose(Sender: Tobject;
var Action: TcloseAction);
begin
  closefile(TRACE_FILE);
  objCOSA.Destroy;
end;
```

The Methods in the Logic Class

The COSA object "objCOSA" is created by a call from the TFormCalc class to the TCOSAcalc class constructor. The logic for the Calculator is created dynamically using the object "objCOSA" to call the "CreateRules" procedure.

```
Procedure TformCalc.CreateCOSA_OnActivate(Sender: Tobject);
begin
  objCOSA := TCOSAcalc.Create;
  objCOSA.CreateRules();
end;
```

The procedure "pMCM" dynamically fills the logic array "rRule" with the defined COSA rules. The "pMCM" procedure defines the structure of the COSA Extended BNF Table to correspond to the structure of the COSA engine.

```
procedure TCOSAcalc.pMCM(iTime : integer; iState : integer;
    pTrueRule : pProcedureType; iTrueRule : integer;
    pFalseRule : pProcedureType; iFalseRule : integer;
    iTrace : integer);
begin
  rRule[iTime] := TCOSARules.Create;
  rRule[iTime].iTime := iTime;
  rRule[iTime].iState := iState;
  rRule[iTime].pTrueRule := pTrueRule;
  rRule[iTime].iTrueRule := iTrueRule;
  rRule[iTime].pFalseRule := pFalseRule;
  rRule[iTime].iFalseRule := iFalseRule;
  rRule[iTime].iTrace := iTrace;
end;
```

61

The procedure "CreateRules" uses the "pMCM" procedure to dynamically create the COSA rules making the rules ready for runtime logic execution.

```
procedure TCOSAcalc.CreateRules();
begin
{$INCLUDE 'Create_Data.inc'}
  rOper1 := 0;                                  // First Operand Rule
  rOper8 := rOper1 + 7;                         // Operation Rules
  rOper2 := rOper8 + 4;                         // Second Operand Rule
  rResult := rOper2 + 8;                        // Result Rules
  rError  := rResult + 3;                       // Error Handler Rules
//              Static   True            Next True    False        Next False
//    Rules     State    Behavior        Rule         Behavior     Rule      Trace
pMCM(rOper1,    iNeg44,  Negate,         rOper1+1,    Ignore,      rOper1+1, 100);
pMCM(rOper1+1,  iDigit,  Any_Number,     rOper1+1,    Ignore,      rOper1+2, 101);
pMCM(rOper1+2,  iDot59,  One_Period,     rOper1+3,    Ignore,      rOper1+4, 102);
pMCM(rOper1+3,  iDigit,  Any_Number,     rOper1+3,    Ignore,      rOper1+4, 103);
pMCM(rOper1+4,  iClEnt,  Clear_Entry,    rOper1,      Ignore,      rOper1+5, 104);
pMCM(rOper1+5,  iClear,  Clear,          rOper1,      Ignore,      rOper1+6, 105);
pMCM(rOper1+6,  iPush,   Push_Disp,      rOper8,      Push_Disp,   rOper8,   106);
// operations
pMCM(rOper8,    iAdd43,  Addition,       rOper2,      Ignore,      rOper8+1, 500);
pMCM(rOper8+1,  iSub44,  Subtraction,    rOper2,      Ignore,      rOper8+2, 501);
pMCM(rOper8+2,  iMul42,  Multiply,       rOper2,      Ignore,      rOper8+3, 502);
pMCM(rOper8+3,  iDiv47,  Division,       rOper2,      Ignore,      rError,   503);
// next number
pMCM(rOper2,    iOff,    Engine_Off,     rOper2+1,    Engine_Off,  rOper2+1, 700);
pMCM(rOper2+1,  iNeg44,  Negate,         rOper2+2,    Ignore,      rOper2+2, 701);
pMCM(rOper2+2,  iDigit,  Any_Number,     rOper2+2,    Ignore,      rOper2+3, 702);
pMCM(rOper2+3,  iDot59,  One_Period,     rOper2+4,    Ignore,      rOper2+5, 703);
pMCM(rOper2+4,  iDigit,  Any_Number,     rOper2+4,    Ignore,      rOper2+5, 704);
// clear
pMCM(rOper2+5,  iClEnt,  Clear_Entry,    rOper2,      Ignore,      rOper2+6, 705);
pMCM(rOper2+6,  iClEnt,  Clear,          rOper2,      Ignore,      rOper2+7, 706);
pMCM(rOper2+7,  iSave,   Save_Disp,      rResult,     Save_Disp,   rResult,  707);
// equals
pMCM(rResult,   iPer37,  Percent,        rOper1,      Ignore,      rResult+1,900);
pMCM(rResult+1, iEqual,  Equals,         rOper1,      Ignore,      rResult+2,901);
pMCM(rResult+2, iChain,  Operate,        rOper8,      Operate,     rOper8,   902);
pMCM(rError,    iErr86,  Unknown,        rOper1,      Error,       rOper1,   993);
end;
```

The following methods are dynamically bound by the engine and are contained in the logic class "TCOSAcalc." The private methods in the data-flow are simple, using no parameters for this particular application. Each method does one thing for the state and does it well.

The "negate" method puts the "-" at the beginning of ASCII number about to be built, and turns the engine off. When the engine is turned off, the display is updated using the following statement:

formCalc.editdisplay.Text := sBuildNumber;

The following procedures "Negate", "Any_Number", and "One_Period" are the three routines that build the first and second operand as strings.

```
procedure TCOSAcalc.Negate();
begin
  sBuildNumber := '-';
  bEngine := FALSE;
end;

procedure TCOSAcalc.Any_Number();
begin
  sBuildNumber := sBuildNumber + sArgValue;
  bEngine := FALSE;
end;

procedure TCOSAcalc.One_Period();
begin
  sBuildNumber := sBuildNumber + sArgValue;
  bEngine := FALSE;
end;
```

The "Any_Number" method concatenates the argument digit with the number being built, and then turns the engine off. The "One_Period" method concatenates a period to the number being built and turns the engine off. The next temporal step is the "Any_Number" at "rOper1+1". The "Any_Number" method is the same as the "rOper1+3", "rOper2+2", and "rOper2+4" steps. Likewise, the "Negate" method at step "rOper2+1" is the same as the "rOper1" step. That is, the first operand rule and the second operand rule use the same code to negate the displayed number.

The following four operations are pseudo operations. At the time they are executed their only role is to set up the proper operation (ADD, SUB, MUL, and DIVN) through the virtual pointer "pOperArg00", which will be dynamically bound and executed when the result rule is traversed. The methods of the "rOper8" rule like "Addition" are contained in trace numbers starting with 500. These are the four valid dynamic operator states allowed in our calculator example:

```
Procedure TCOSAcalc.Addition();
begin
  pOperArg00 := ADD;     //place addr addition in dynamic bind
end;

Procedure TCOSAcalc.Subtraction();
begin
  pOperArg00 := SUB;     //place addr subtract in dynamic bind
end;



Procedure TCOSAcalc.Multiply();
begin
  pOperArg00 := MUL;     //place addr multiply in dynamic bind
end;

Procedure TCOSAcalc.Division();
begin
  pOperArg00 := DIVN;    //place addr divide in dynamic bind
end;
```

The second operand methods are the same as the first operand, except the "Push_Disp" method replaces the "Save_Disp" method. The methods of the "Result" rule, "Percent", "Operate", and "Equal", are orthogonal operations on the two entered values.

The "Percent" procedure sets up the "PERC" procedure for a dynamic call within the try/except. The percent operation is executed when the percent button is clicked. If the operation doesn't fail, the "sBuildNumber" is loaded with the result. If the operation does fail, then the exception is displayed.

```
procedure TCOSAcalc.Percent();
 begin
 pOperArg00 := PERC;      // setup dynamic bind
 try
    pOperArg00();          // dynamic call
      sbuildNumber := FloatToStr(fNumber);
 except
 sbuildNumber:= 'Not A Number.';
  dynamicState := 86;   // not Maxwell Smart
  end;
 engLocal := FALSE;
 end;
```

The mathematics in the percent statement is a little different from the other four operators. The "Percent" operation takes the result number and multiplies it by the entered percent divided by 100.

```
Procedure TCOSAcalc.PERC();
begin
   fNumber := fNumber * (1.0 + fDisplay/100.0);
end;
```

The "Operate" method at trace 902 must find an operation rather than a percent or equal to allow it to continue operating on the result as in "8 + 5 * 9 / 2 + 23 - 1.4 =". Until the equal sign button is clicked, the operation can continue to chain.

```
procedure TCOSAcalc.Operate();
 begin
  sBuildNumber := '0';
 try
    pOperArg00();          // bind to last operator
     sbuildNumber := FloatToStr(fNumber);
 except
 sbuildNumber:= 'Not A Number.';
     dynamicState := 86;   // not Maxwell Smart
   end;
 end;
```

The "Equals" method calls the dynamically bound generic method that is performing the correct operation between the first operand and the second operand and places the result in the display.

```
procedure TCOSAcalc.Equals();
begin
  formCalc.sNumber := '';
  try
  pOperArg00();              // call dynamically bound operation
    sbuildNumber := FloatToStr(fNumber);
  fNumber := 0.0;
except
  sbuildNumber:= 'Divide by Zero.';
  dynamicState := 86;        // not Maxwell Smart
  end;
engLocal := FALSE;
end;
```

Operand 1 builds the string variable "sNumber". When an operation is entered, the string contained in "sNumber" is converted to a floating-point number contained in "fNumber". Then operand 2 builds in the string "sNumber" until a result is selected, causing "sNumber" to be converted to "fDisplay". The math looks like this:

fNumber = fNumber **operation** fDisplay

"fNumber" is then put into the "sDisplay" and displayed in the calculator as the result. In a chain operation, the "sNumber" and "fDisplay" continue to be used until an equal operation is entered.

The following four functions are executed through the dynamic binding call "pOperArg00( )" when the equal button is clicked. The traditional ITE uses a similar approach in C++ that looks like "(this➔*method())" in its "Dispatch()" function.

66

```
Procedure TCOSAcalc.MUL();
begin
  fNumber := fNumber * fDisplay;
end;

procedure TCOSAcalc.DIVN();
begin
  fNumber := fNumber / fDisplay;
end;

procedure TCOSAcalc.ADD();
begin
  fNumber := fNumber + fDisplay;
end;

procedure TCOSAcalc.SUB();
begin
  fNumber := fNumber - fDisplay;
end;
```

The "Push_Disp" at trace 106 is called after the first operand has been entered. The calculator application manages the numbers as they are built behind the scenes. The try/except handles issues of "Not a Number," which can happen when operations are entered with no number or other operator maladies.

```
Procedure TCOSAcalc.Push_Disp();
begin
  try
  fNumber := StrToFloat(sBuildNumber);
  sBuildNumber := '';
  except
  dynamicState := 86;    // Max again
  bEngine := FALSE;
  sBuildNumber := 'Not a Number.';
  end;
end;
```

The "Save_Disp" at trace 707 is called after the second operand has been entered in anticipation of a call to "Percent", "Equals", or "Operate". At this point in time the first

67

operand is held in the variable "fNumber" and the second operand is held in the variable "fDisplay". The first and second operand rules use the same procedures up to the point where the entered strings are converted to floating point numbers.

```
procedure TCOSAcalc.Save_Disp();
begin
  try
  fDisplay := StrToFloat(sBuildNumber);
  sBuildNumber := '0';
  except
  dynamicState := 86;    // and yet again
  bEngine := FALSE;
  sBuildNumber := 'Not a Number.';
  end;
end;
```

The administrative task of controlling the engine is by a simple Boolean state "bEngine" being turned on and off.

```
Procedure TCOSAcalc.Engine_Off();
begin
  bEngine := FALSE;
end;
```

The "CE" button only needs to clear the "sBuildNumber." The "sBuildNumber" is the operand being built.

```
Procedure TCOSAcalc.Clear_Entry();
begin
  sBuildNumber := '0';
  bEngine := FALSE;
end;
```

The Power of Temporal Logic

Setting the "fNumber" to floating point zero is not necessary because "fNumber" is overwritten as a part of the data manipulation in all of the procedures that create the value "fNumber." All of the procedures that use "fNumber" to accumulate can't be reached after a "Clear_Entry" or "Clear" without going through one of the procedures that create the value and thereby overwrite the previous value. The following is a partial COSA Extended BNF Table showing the first operand logic for reference.

```
//                              Next                Next
//Rule      Static   True       True     False      False
//Step      State    Actions    Rule     Actions    Rule       Trace
// Operand 1
rOper1,     iNeg44,  Negate,    rOper1+1, Ignore,   rOper1+1,  100
rOper1+1,   iDigit,  Any_Number, rOper1+1, Ignore,  rOper1+2,  101
rOper1+2,   iDot59,  One_Period, rOper1+3, Ignore,  rOper1+4,  102
rOper1+3,   iDigit,  Any_Number, rOper1+3, Ignore,  rOper1+4,  103
rOper1+4,   iClEnt,  Clear_Entry, rOper1,  Ignore,  rOper1+5,  104
rOper1+5,   iClear,  Clear,     rOper1,   Ignore,   rOper1+6,  105
rOper1+6,   iPush,   Push_Disp, rOper8,   Push_Disp rOper8,    106
```
Table 6.0
First Operand Logic

The real difference between "Clear_Entry" and "Clear" is in the execution of the temporal logic. When the button CE is clicked the temporal logic in "rOper1" returns "iTime" to the operand rule at "rOper1". The temporal logic at the use of "Clear" returns "iTime" to the first operand rule "rOper1" also. So, for the *first* operand rule, the procedures "Clear_Entry" and "Clear" could be the same.

```
Procedure TCOSAcalc.Clear();
begin
   fNumber := 0.0;         // not necessary.
   sBuildNumber := '0';
   bEngine := FALSE;
end;
```

The second operand logic is repeated below. When the button CE is clicked the temporal logic in "rOper2" returns "iTime" to the operand rule at "rOper2". The temporal logic in "rOper2" at the use of "Clear" returns "iTime" to the first operand rule "rOper1" just like "Clear" in "rOper1". So for the *second* operand rule the procedures "Clear_Entry" and "Clear" are *also* the same.

//
//Rule
//Step
	Static
	State
		True
		Actions
			Next
			True
			Rule
				False
				Actions
					Next
					False
					Rule
						Trace

// Operand 2						
rOper2,	iOff,	Engine_Off,	rOper2+1,	Eng_Off,	rOper2+1,	700
rOper2+1,	iNeg44,	Negate,	rOper2+2,	Ignore,	rOper2+2,	701
rOper2+2,	iDigit,	Any_Number,	rOper2+2,	Ignore,	rOper2+3,	702
rOper2+3,	iDot59,	One_Period,	rOper2+4,	Ignore,	rOper2+5,	703
rOper2+4,	iDigit,	Any_Number,	rOper2+4,	Ignore,	rOper2+5,	704
rOper2+5,	iClEnt,	Clear_Entry,	**rOper2+1,**	Ignore,	rOper2+6,	705
rOper2+6,	iClear,	Clear,	**rOper1,**	Ignore,	rOper2+7,	706
rOper2+7,	iSave,	Save_Disp,	rResult,	Save_Disp	rResult,	707

Table 6.1
Second Operand Logic

The logic is the only difference between the procedures "Clear_Entry" and "Clear". These two routines can be combined into one, reducing the size of the application. These discoveries are important to engineers working in real-time where cycles count; they are a lot easier to find when the logic is separate from the data manipulation.

The GUI Form Class

The Borland / Delphi developer environment makes this part of experimenting fairly easy. The variables beginning with "TformCalc" down to the "private" are all generated from the drag and drop process of creating the calculator form. The task of connecting the GUI to the logic is very simple, each "on-click" event calls the COSA Engine.

```
TformCalc = class(Tform)
  panelMain: Tpanel;
  tabPageControl: TpageControl;
  tabCalculator: TtabSheet;
  editDisplay: Tedit;
  tabTraceLogic: TtabSheet;
  listStateDisplay: TlistBox;
  Button7: Tbutton;
  Button8: Tbutton;
  Button9: Tbutton;
  ButtonC: Tbutton;
  ButtonCE: Tbutton;
  ButtonSubtract: Tbutton;
  ButtonDivide: Tbutton;
  ButtonPercent: Tbutton;
  ButtonEquals: Tbutton;
  ButtonMultiply: Tbutton;
  ButtonAddition: Tbutton;
  ButtonPeriod: Tbutton;
  Button3: Tbutton;
  Button6: Tbutton;
  Button0: Tbutton;
  Button2: Tbutton;
  Button5: Tbutton;
  Button1: Tbutton;
  Button4: Tbutton;


  procedure SelectZero_OnClick(Sender: Tobject);
  procedure SelectOne_OnClick(Sender: Tobject);
  procedure SelectTwo_OnClick(Sender: Tobject);
  procedure SelectThree_OnClick(Sender: Tobject);
  procedure SelectFour_OnClick(Sender: Tobject);
  procedure SelectFive_OnClick(Sender: Tobject);
  procedure SelectSix_OnClick(Sender: Tobject);
```

```
procedure SelectSeven_OnClick(Sender: Tobject);
procedure SelectEight_OnClick(Sender: Tobject);
procedure SelectNine_OnClick(Sender: Tobject);
procedure CreateCOSA_OnActivate(Sender: Tobject);
procedure SelectClear_OnClick(Sender: Tobject);
procedure SelectClearEntry_OnClick(Sender: Tobject);
procedure SelectAddition_OnClick(Sender: Tobject);
procedure SelectSubtraction_OnClick(Sender: Tobject);
procedure SelectMultiply_OnClick(Sender: Tobject);
procedure SelectEquals_OnClick(Sender: Tobject);
procedure SelectPercent_OnClick(Sender: Tobject);
procedure SelectPeriod_OnClick(Sender: Tobject);
procedure SelectDivide_OnClick(Sender: Tobject);
procedure CloseTraceFile_OnClose(Sender: Tobject;
    var Action: TcloseAction);

private
    { Private declarations }
    rCalc, rErr, rDone : integer;
    dynamicState, iTime : Integer;
    sNumber, sDisplay : String;
public
    { Public declarations }
    objCOSA : TCOSAcalc;
end;
```

TformCalc Class

The COSA Calculator Class

The TCOSAcalc is the work class with all of the logic defined in the COSA Extended BNF Table (Extended BNF). Interface access is granted through the procedure "Run". The "Run" procedure provides the "on-click" state and an ASCII character to the engine. A point of note is the "pOperArg00" : "pProcedureType" definition. This is used to dynamically bind the proper operation when the equal sign is clicked.

Another point of note is the "rRule : Array of type TCOSArules". This array contains the rules defined by the Extended BNF.

```
    rOper1, rOper8, rOper2, rResult, rError : integer;
```

The row addresses are defined by the rules in the Extended BNF. The first row "rOper1" is set to zero. Rule "rOper1" has seven physical states. The "rOper8" is defined as "rOper1" plus 7. The rule "rOper2" is defined as "rOper8" plus 4. Whenever a row is added to a rule, the base of the following rule must be updated. For example, if a square root rule is added to "rOper8", then the "rOper2" rule would have five steps. And rule "rOper2" would be defined as "rOper8" plus 5.

```
procedure TCOSAcalc.CreateRules();
begin
{$INCLUDE 'Create_Data.inc'}
  rOper1 := 0;                              // First Operand Rule
  rOper8 := rOper1 + 7;                     // Operation Rules
  rOper2 := rOper8 + 4;                     // Second Operand Rule
  rResult := rOper2 + 8;                    // Result Rules
  rError  := rResult + 3;                   // Error Handler Rules
        o o o
```

COSA Extend BNF Rules table goes here…

```
//*********** COSA Framework for Rules to Run In **********
  TCOSAcalc = class(TCOSARules)      // inherits from
  public
  constructor Create;
  destructor Destroy; override;
  procedure Run(intState : integer; sNumber : String);
  private
  dynamicState, iIndex : integer;
  iAdd43, iSub44, iMul42 : integer;         // Static States
  iDiv47, iPer37, iNeg44 : integer;         // Static States
  iDigit, iDot59, iClEnt : integer;         // Static States
  iPush, iSave, iChain, iOFF : integer;     // Static States
  iClear, iErr86, iEqual : integer;         // Static States
  rOper1, rOper8, rOper2, rResult, rError : integer;
  bEngine : boolean;
  fNumber, fDisplay, fTrace : real;
  pOperArg00 : pProcedureType;              // FOR DYNAMIC BINDING
  sReturnDisplay, sBuildNumber : String;
  strTrueBehavior : Array [0..22] of String;
  strFalseBehavior : Array [0..22] of String;
  rRule : Array [0..22] of TCOSARules;      // COSA Extended BNF
RULES
  TRACE_FILE : TextFile;
```

```
private
  procedure pMCM(iTime : integer; iState : integer;
           pTrueRule : pProcedureType; iTrueRule : integer;
           pFalseRule : pProcedureType; iFalseRule : integer;
           iTrace : integer);

  procedure MUL();
  procedure DIVN();      // div is a reserved word in Delphi
  procedure ADD();
  procedure SUB();
  procedure PERC();

     procedure True_Trace(iTime : integer);
     procedure False_Trace(iTime : integer);

  procedure CreateRules();
  procedure Error();
  procedure Ignore();

  procedure Clear();
  procedure Clear_Entry();

  procedure Negate();         // builds negative number
  procedure Any_Number();     // build integer and fraction
  procedure One_Period();     // adds decimal point

  procedure Push_Disp();
  procedure Engine_Off();
  procedure Save_Disp();
  procedure Done();

  procedure Addition();
  procedure Subtraction();
  procedure Multiply();
  procedure Division();

  procedure Percent();
  procedure Operate();
  procedure Equals();

  procedure Unknown();
  end;
```

The COSA Rules Class

The TCOSARules class defines the column structure for the Extended BNF Rules Table. The first line after the comment

"pProcedureType = **procedure** of Object;"

is the definition that allows the application to dynamically bind at runtime to the true and false behaviors. The "iTime" definition is a vestigial column as the comment says. In a table it is only used as a placeholder to show the step-row location. When the rules are created dynamically in the "CreateRules" method the rule base "rOper1" is set to zero.

```
// ******************** COSA Rules Definition ******************
  pProcedureType = procedure of Object;
  fButtonType = function : Tobject;
  TCOSARules = class
  public
  private
  iTime : integer;      // Temporal Component (vestigial place keeper)
  iState : integer;                 // Expected State Value
  pTrueRule : pProcedureType;       // True Behavior
  iTrueRule : integer;              // Next iTime on True
  pFalseRule : pProcedureType;      // False Behavior
  iFalseRule : integer;             // Next iTime on False
  iTrace : integer;                 // Trace Value or Code
  end;
```

The second column is the static state definition. The third column is the true behavior definition. The forth column is the definition for next true temporal transition. The fifth column is the false behavior definition. The sixth column defines the next false temporal transition. The last column is the trace type.

Summary

This chapter covers the procedures that manipulate the data. There are three complex procedures. First is the run procedure that contains the engine. Second is the procedure that creates the rules. The rules structure for the COSA Extended BNF Table is defined as a class. Each row of the COSA Extend BNF class is dynamically created and placed in an array in the pMCM procedure. The third complex procedure is the group of results procedures.

The framework provided by Borland makes access to the Windows operating system easy. Using Delphi's drag and drop approach it is very easy to create the user calculator interface. Creating the "on-click" events provide the interface to the logic. Borland, in their Delphi implementation, have a naming convention that I have tried to follow in this text. It is important to label every variable with a prefix-Polish notation. This approach allows code manufacture to use the same name, creating a relationship.

7

Chapter 7 – COSA Trace

Once an application has begun testing the ability to trace the execution of the logic could be a paramount task. In the design of an application, testing should always be a consideration. Even if trace is designed into an application, enormous efforts can be required to get the right information about the runtime application. The spatial approach to application implementation, with the distributed "if-then-else" logic throughout the application, makes the task of a comprehensive trace almost impossible at design time or after the fact. The COSA trace has solved this very complex problem.

The COSA implementation includes an integral trace as a part of the architecture. With trace integral to the architecture, the trace of documentation and runtime considerations are handled to a greater level of detail than many standards require. With the separation of software components into engine, rules table, and procedures, the trace documentation can specify exactly where a change or problem occurred. For example, trace documentation can explain that the logic was changed to handle additional use cases. And, because the logic is separate from the data manipulation the new use cases may not require any changes to the supporting procedures.

Another feature of integral trace is the ability of a help-mechanism to understand the flow of logic that put a particular user in a specific part of the application's logic. This kind of tracking information can be valuable for understanding consumer logic, user logic, or hacker logic. Systems will become more secure when temporal logic is built into them.

The COSA Extended BNF Table is repeated here to help with the analysis of dynamic trace that follows.

Rule	Static State	True Behavior	Next True Rule	False Behavior	Next False Rule	Trace
// Operand 1						
rOper1,	iNeg44,	Negate,	rOper1+1,	Ignore,	rOper1+1,	100
rOper1+1,	iDigit,	Any_Number	rOper1+1,	Ignore,	rOper1+2,	101
rOper1+2,	iDot59,	One_Period	rOper1+3,	Ignore,	rOper1+4,	102
rOper1+3,	iDigit,	Any_Number	rOper1+3,	Ignore,	rOper1+4,	103
rOper1+4,	iClEnt,	Clear_Entry	rOper1,	Ignore,	rOper1+5,	104
rOper1+5,	iClear,	Clear,	rOper1,	Ignore,	rOper1+6,	105
rOper1+6,	iPush,	Push_Disp,	rOper8,	Push_Disp,	rOper8,	106
// Operation						
rOper8,	iAdd43,	Addition,	rOper2,	Ignore,	rOper8+1,	500
rOper8+1,	iSub44,	Subtraction,	rOper2,	Ignore,	rOper8+2,	501
rOper8+2,	iMul42,	Multiply,	rOper2,	Ignore,	rOper8+3,	502
rOper8+3,	iDiv47,	Division,	rOper2,	Ignore,	rError,	503
// Operand 2						
rOper2,	iOff,	Engine_Off	rOper2+1,	Eng_Off,	rOper2+1,	700
rOper2+1,	iNeg44,	Negate,	rOper2+2,	Ignore,	rOper2+2,	701
rOper2+2,	iDigit,	Any_Number	rOper2+2,	Ignore,	rOper2+3,	702
rOper2+3,	iDot59,	One_Period	rOper2+4,	Ignore,	rOper2+5,	703
rOper2+4,	iDigit,	Any_Number	rOper2+4,	Ignore,	rOper2+5,	704
rOper2+5,	iClEnt,	Clear_Entry	rOper2+1,	Ignore,	rOper2+6,	705
rOper2+6,	iClear,	Clear,	rOper1,	Ignore,	rOper2+7,	706
rOper2+7,	iSave,	Save_Disp,	rResult,	Save_Disp,	rResult,	707
// Result						
rResult,	iPer37,	Percent,	rOper1,	Ignore,	rResult+1,	900
rResult+1,	iEqual,	Equals,	rOper1,	Ignore,	rResult+2,	901
rResult+2,	iChain,	Operate,	rOper8,	Operate,	rOper8,	902
rError,	iErr86,	Unknown,	rOper1,	Error,	rOper1,	993

Table 7.0
COSA Extended BNF Rules Table

Toward Fully Automated Testing

A testing scenario can be forecast from the final BNF (Tree 5.1) using the trace numbers that have been assigned. When the tests are run through the application the testing scenario should match the trace file. The test analysis file will look like final BNF with the trace numbers replacing the elements: <100>? <101>* (<102> <103>+)? … This test analysis file allows for all possible scenarios that have been designed into the application. This approach also allows for the automatic generation of the test file since the individual states are coherent. The test generator knows to generate a negate "<100>?" in one scenario, zero or more integer-portions "<101>*" in another scenario, and optional decimal portions "(<102><103>+)?" in another scenario.

Using the COSA approach to testing the location of source bugs[34] can be found faster and with more precision as the next few pages reveal. The COSA engine provides a centralized trace for each object than can be turned on and off or changed (dynamically bound) to different trace objects as needed, and each centralized trace can be customized to provide any level of detail to help with testing and debugging. The testing tools can include the generation of process maps to help understand performance density where logic or data tuning might help performance.

The potential cost reduction from an improved testing infrastructure, according to the referenced NIST paper (section 8-6), is $22.249 billion in 2002 dollars. Any improvement in testing is important to the quality of software. That number is interesting because it is only about one-third of the $59.5 billion 2002 dollars the industry looses due to bugs.

---

[34] Gregory Tassey, "The Economic Impacts of Inadequate Infrastructure for Software Testing", May 2002, National Institute of Standards and Technology, Section 4.1.3, Page 4.3

The Ultimate Dynamic Trace

COSA trace can be as simple or elaborate as the testing requires. In this example everything of interest in the calculator example has been added to the trace. Entering "-3.14159" results in the engine generating the following temporal trace:

```
T/F   Rule+   Engine   Static    Dynamic   Behavior       Trace   Result
+T    0;      Off;     S= 44;    D= 44;    Negate;        100     N= -
+T    1;      Off;     S=  1;    D=  1;    Any_Number;    101     N= -3
-F    1;      On;      S=  1;    D= 59;    Ignore;        101     N= -3
+T    2;      Off;     S= 59;    D= 59;    One_Period;    102     N= -3.
+T    3;      Off;     S=  1;    D=  1;    Any_Number;    103     N= -3.1
+T    3;      Off;     S=  1;    D=  1;    Any_Number;    103     N= -3.14
+T    3;      Off;     S=  1;    D=  1;    Any_Number;    103     N= -3.141
+T    3;      Off;     S=  1;    D=  1;    Any_Number;    103     N= -3.1415
+T    3;      Off;     S=  1;    D=  1;    Any_Number;    103     N= -3.14159
```
Trace 7.0
Calculator Operand 1

The engine is turned off and control is returned to the OS message loop after every step where the Engine column shows "Off". The third line of Trace 7.0 starts with –F, indicating a false behavior, the Engine column shows the engine remained "On". The control-flow logic is looking for a static state "1", the number building step. But the dynamic state had a value of 59, which is a period. The engine remained on and time moved to the next true step at Trace 102, the period static state value of 59. Satisfied with a match between static and dynamic, the engine is turned off. The trace example shows that step "rOper1+3", in *Table 7.0* on the previous page, of the first rule is repeatedly executed, and the "Trace" column shows that trace 103 is repeated five times. As long as a number is entered, the fractional portion of the number is built. This would also apply to step "rOper +1" in *Table 7.0* when building the integer portion of the number.

The next part of the example for the engine is to perform a subtraction operation by clicking on the "-". This results in the "on-click" event handler catching the operation and returning to the "temporal" location left by the previous operation.

In the following Trace 7.1, the first five events in the first column are false. There isn't a match at static values "S= 1","S= 12", "S= 11," "S= 1", and "S= 43", and only their false behaviors were executed. In the logic table these steps correspond to ending the concatenation of numbers that were building the fractional part of the number and looking for the operation. The column labeled Dynamic contains the "D= 44," which is the ASCII code for "-" (subtraction).

The true next step follows the "Subtraction" operation directly to the "Engine_Off" temporal trace number 700 in Trace 7.1 to allow the engine to be turned off. Control is returned to the "on click" event handler and back to the Windows message loop for the next event to be trapped.

T/F	Rule+	Engine	Static	Dynamic	Behavior	Trace	Result
-F	3;	On;	S= 1;	D= 44;	Ignore;	103	N= -3.14159
-F	4;	On;	S= 12;	D= 44;	Ignore;	104	N= -3.14159
-F	5;	On;	S= 11;	D= 44;	Ignore;	105	N= -3.14159
-F	6;	On;	S= 1;	D= 44;	Push_Disp;	106	N= -3.14159
-F	7;	On;	S= 43;	D= 44;	Ignore;	500	N= -3.14159
+T	8;	On;	S= 44;	D= 1;	Subtract;	501	N= -3.14159
+T	11;	Off;	S= 1;	D= 1;	Eng_Off;	700	N= -3.14159

Trace 7.1

Calculator Operation

In the Trace 7.2, the number "-2.14159" is entered. The second operand rule "rOper2", from *Table 7.0*, performs the same as the first operand rule. The second operand is built and displayed just as the first operand was built and displayed. Trace goes from 701 to 704. At 704 the trace is repeated, building the fractional part of the number.

T/F	Rule+	Engine	Static	Dynamic	Behavior	Trace	Result
+T	12;	Off;	S= 44;	D= 44;	Negate;	701;	N= -
+T	13;	Off;	S= 1;	D= 1;	Any_Number;	702;	N= -2
-F	13;	On;	S= 1;	D= 59;	Ignore;	702;	N= -2
+T	14;	Off;	S= 59;	D= 59;	One_Period;	703;	N= -2.
+T	15;	Off;	S= 1;	D= 1;	Any_Number;	704;	N= -2.1
+T	15;	Off;	S= 1;	D= 1;	Any_Number;	704;	N= -2.14
+T	15;	Off;	S= 1;	D= 1;	Any_Number;	704;	N= -2.141
+T	15;	Off;	S= 1;	D= 1;	Any_Number;	704;	N= -2.1415
+T	15;	Off;	S= 1;	D= 1;	Any_Number;	704;	N= -2.14159

Trace 7.2
Calculator Operand 2

When the equal sign is clicked, the proper "on-click" event handler calls the engine again starting at "rOper2+4", in *Table 7.0*. Since the dynamic state is looking for a token of value "13," the engine transitions from trace 704 through to trace 901. In *Table 7.0* this is in rule "rResult" at step 1. The result is then displayed, and the next true rule is back to "rOper1," which is back at the beginning of the logic in *Table 7.0*.

T/F	Rule+	Engine	Static	Dynamic	Behavior	Trace	Result
-F	15;	On;	S= 1;	D= 13;	Ignore;	**704;**	N= -2.14159
-F	16;	On;	S= 12;	D= 13;	Ignore;	705;	N= -2.14159
-F	17;	On;	S= 11;	D= 13;	Ignore;	706;	N= -2.14159
-F	18;	On;	S= 1;	D= 13;	Save_Disp;	707;	N= -2.14159
-F	19;	On;	S= 37;	D= 13;	Ignore;	900;	N= -2.14159
+T	20;	Off	S= 13;	D= 13;	Equals;	**901;**	N= -1

Trace 7.3
Calculator Results

The column labeled Behavior was added to the calculator application trace to provide a string listing of the behavior in addition to the trace number. A word compared to a number, when it comes to debugging logic, can be very valuable. When it comes to understanding the logic for debugging, it is useful to display the behavior in the trace: "a picture is worth a thousand words".

Dynamic Trace in the Application

The next few pages show a series of screen shots of the calculator and dynamic trace in action as the calculation of subtracting a negative number from a negative number is performed.

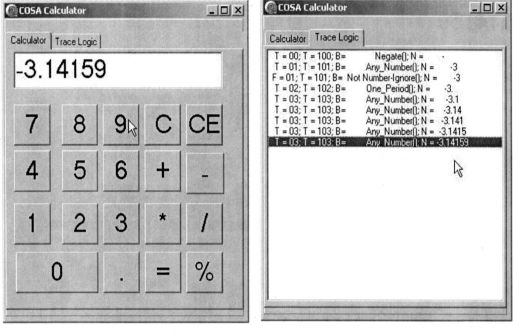

Figure 7.0   **Figure 7.1**

The negative number "-3.14159" is entered in Figure 7.0 creating the trace logic in Figure 7.1. The first column/value in Figure 7.1 is the True or False State displayed as a "T" or an "F." The second value is the temporal step displayed as "00", "01", "02", "03", etc, and the third value is the trace "T = 100" that is coded for each section going back to the specification: 100 for the first operand, 500 for the operator, 700 for the second operand, and 900 for the result rule. The fourth value is the string name of the behavior executed, and the last value in this particular implementation is the intermediate string value as it is built.

As the arithmetic operation continues, the last column displays the operand value built which includes the "-" subtraction operation when it is entered at "T= 12".

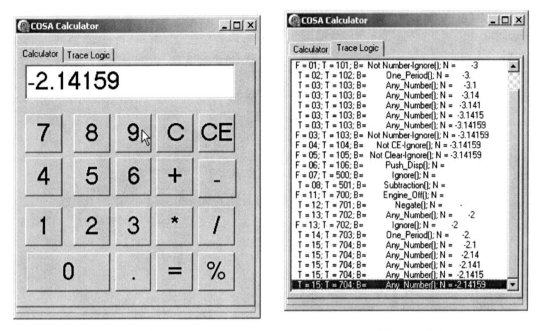

| Figure 7.2 | Figure 7.3 |

The number "-2.14519" has been entered in Figure 7.2. The operational trace in Figure 7.3 shows the actions of subtracting a negative number from the previous negative number.

Notice the skip chain logic from temporal step "F= 03" with "B= Not Number-Ignore" to "T= 08" with "B= Subtraction". This sequence of *not* logic is the engine looking for a match between the dynamic state and the static state which it finds at "T= 08". (In this trace the dynamic and static values are not shown.) The logic skips over the other two operators, multiply (this would have been at "T= 09") and divide (this would have been at "T= 10"), then turns the calculator engine off at "T= 11" with the explicit method of "B= Engine_Off".

84

Figure 7.4 shows the negative one (-1) result of subtracting a negative number from a negative number. The trace in Figure 7.5 of subtracting a negative number from a negative number is complete. As can be seen from this example, the trace can be extremely rich in its content. And since each engine has its own trace routines, it is easy to add or remove information relevant to the class or the object and its inheritance.

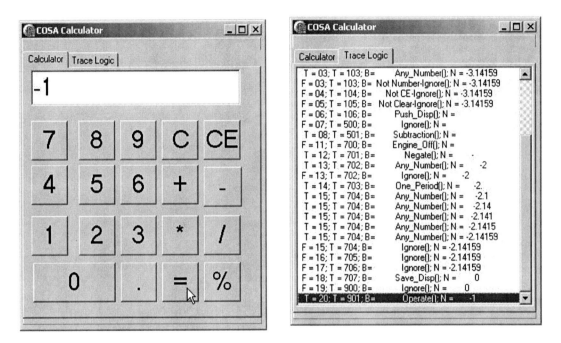

Figure 7.4   **Figure 7.5**

In a temporal approach implemented in a fully commercial GUI, the engineer can look at the UML class diagrams, the state diagrams, the BNF, and the COSA logic-flow and data-flow and be able to interact with trace in the animation of this whole process.

Since the trace files can be very large it would be wise to provide full search capabilities to help in the debugging process.

The Ultimate Static Trace

To comply with various standards like Good Manufacturing Practice (GMP), ISO, DOD-Military and others, any changes made to software must be recorded. The COSA trace facility greatly enhances recording defects and tracking changes. The trace element in each row of the COSA Extended BNF Rules Table provides a common point of reference. When any aspect of the application changes, the details are recorded at the logic level associated with each row. Recording defects and changes in an ITE application is difficult because a common point of reference is not available.

Summary

The COSA dynamic trace provides 100% coverage of the application's logic and can easily be turned on and off. The detail available to COSA static trace exceeds most recording standards for software changes. COSA trace can dramatically improve the quality of the automated testing because the rules/steps provide proof of coverage in an architecture that reduces complexity to logic and the correctness of data manipulation as totally orthogonal components. Plus the BNF and the trace number can be used to design the test suite.

The first seven chapters have introduced COSA as a powerful paradigm for specifying the rules of how to handle the dynamic behavior of reactive objects. Reactive objects are objects that respond to events, like the "on-click events", sent from other objects. The response of a COSA reactive object to an event depends on what rule and iTime the object is in when that the event occurred.

8

Chapter 8 – COSA vs. ITE – Flow Analysis of Procedure Calls

The analysis of the procedure calls within these two vastly different implementations of the five-function calculator gives more insight to the differences between the spatial "If-Then-Else" approach to programming and the temporal COSA.

The COSA implementation of the calculator call analysis is shown in Figure 8.0. Notice that most of the calls are made directly from the run engine. The exception is where the operations are dynamically bound in the "Percent", "Equals", and "Operate" methods. An interesting observation is the COSA call diagram is very similar to the COSA state diagram. The similarity of the logic associated with the application comes from the dynamically bound COSA Extended BNF Rules Table. The call sequence really is the state diagram but it lacks the temporal component. The state diagram shows each time a state is used, whereas, the call diagram only shows one use of a spatial state. Spatially, the "Any_Number" procedure is called from the runtime engine only once, even though temporally, the "Any_Number" routine is called four times as can be seen in the state diagram and COSA Extended BNF.

The temporal organization of this application is simple when compared to the complex spatial approach employed by traditional ITE software. A commercial tool[35] was used to extract the necessary information to create these call diagrams in Microsoft

---

[35] CDOC Documentation Tool for C, C++ and Java, www.swbs.com and www.softwareblacksmiths.com using a feature called CCALL ™ caller/called hierarchy ("flow structure") between functions.

Visio. A call analysis was performed for both applications. The reports shown in Appendix A and B can be used to verify the call structure and relationships.

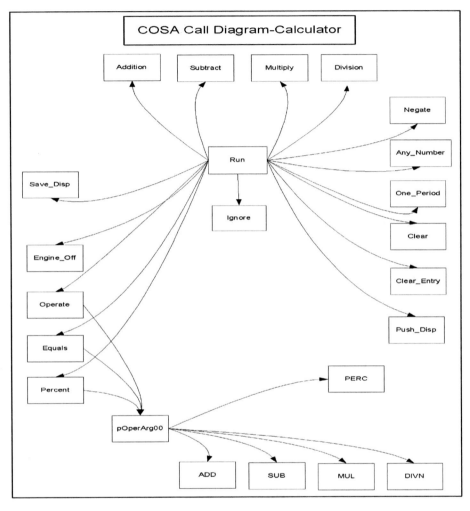

Figure 8.0
COSA Calculator Call Diagram

Figure 8.0 shows the temporal call diagram. Each of the routines may be called multiple times from the engine at the appropriate point in time based on the COSA logic table. The procedure "Negate" is used by both rules for the first and second operand.

The only procedures that are unique between the first and second operand rules is the "Save_Disp" and the "Push_Disp" routines.

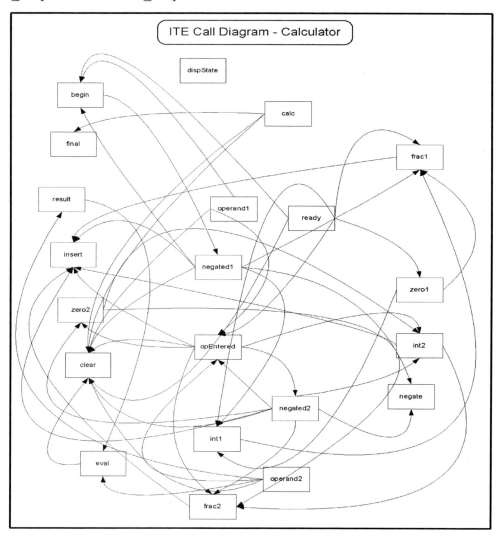

Figure 8.1
ITE Calculator Call Diagram

Graphically, Figure 8.1 represents a spatial call diagram of the ITE calculator. The complexity of this diagram comes from the need of the event to determine its state in the application. For example, the procedure "begin" is called from "ready" and "operand1."

90

In the process of building the number "frac1"is called by "negated1," "ready," and "zero1." The procedure "insert" on the left of the diagram is called six times from six different procedures. The procedure "calc" doesn't show a call arrow but it is called from inside "begin" using a macro. The generalized ITE coding technique is difficult to understand, generate, secure, maintain, or improve without causing side effects and bugs.

Trace has been added to the temporal COSA in Figure 8.2. It's the two dashed lines running from the Run engine to the trace boxes. Trace coverage is 100% of all procedures called.

Testing the ITE Approach

According to a NIST report[36] the software industry spent one-third of its revenue fixing its products. Even so Bill Gates[37] once bragged; if cars were produced like software they would cost less and get much better gas mileage. While that maybe true on the surface it does not speak to the quality of software. The NIST report points out that 302,450 Full Time Equivalent software engineers and computer programmers were engaged in fixing bugs every year. Considering that Figure 8.1 represents the standard for the software referenced in the NIST report one can see why so much time is spent debugging. But NIST refers to an inadequate infrastructure for software testing when in fact the industry has built a massive infrastructure around an ITE basis, which, realistically can't be tested adequately. The report goes on to point out that up to $22 billion could be saved from infrastructure testing improvements.

---

[36] Gregory Tassey, "The Economic Impacts of Inadequate Infrastructure for Software Testing", May 2002, National Institute of Standards and Technology. Chapter 8, "National Impact Estiamtes"
[37] An urban legend starts http://www.snopes.com/humor/jokes/autos.asp about GM response.

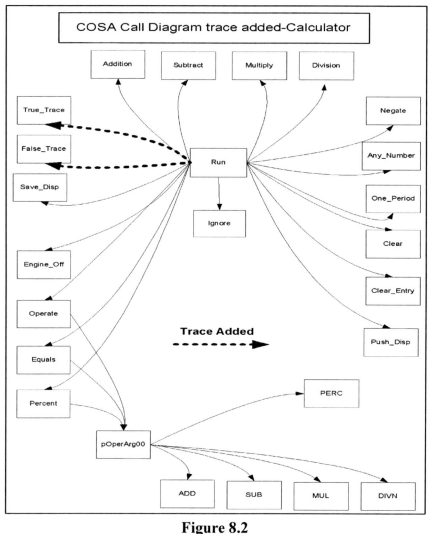

Figure 8.2
COSA Calculator Call Diagram with Trace Added

Both of these applications have been implemented using an object approach. Both applications provide the same functionality, but clearly there is a difference. The logic in COSA is temporal and produces organized diagrams. The logic in the traditional ITE spatial approach appears unorganized in this application. Trace in Figure 8.3 has been added to the ITE approach but it still doesn't provide full coverage with several procedures ("eval", "clear", "zero2", and "negate") not called because it would make the diagram unreadable.

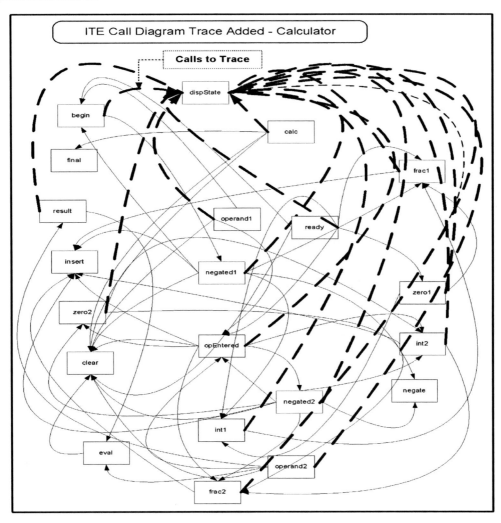

Figure 8.3
ITE Calculator Call Diagram with Trace Added

The complexity in Figure 8.3 is not artificial. There is no way to reduce the complexity of diagram by moving the procedures around because the definitions are spatial. The complexity is inherent in the ITE approach. Assuming that these two approaches (temporal and spatial) remain true to their inherent nature, one can see how billions of dollars[38] can be spent on software bugs using the ITE approach. Clearly, bad logic can create problems and complexity for any approach, but COSA provides an approach that is grounded in binary and temporal logic. Even good logic is difficult to understand using the ITE approach. In an ITE application complexity can't be reduced because the engineer can't do one simple piece of logic. With ITE, adding any other functionality to a procedure increases the complexity of that procedure. With COSA, added functionality can be achieved through changing the Extended BNF Table logic without changing any procedure.

An Efficiency Comparison with ITE

With ITE the application does not have an inherent temporal component. Any ITE application must repeatedly test to determine where in the state sequence the execution is working. Referring back to the ITE state diagram of Figure 4.3 the "negated1" (3) state is entered six times. This can be seen in the ITE Trace[39] Table 8.0 below between sequence 13 and 27. The "int1" (6) state is entered six times in the trace sequence between 23 and 36. The "frac1" (7) state is entered ten times in the trace sequence between 34 and 47. The traditional ITE approach never knows what event may occur next. Therefore the design of an application must consider every possible event to call itself robust.

To enter the first operand "-3.14159" the ITE trace Table 8.0 below is shown in trace sequence 13 through to 48 where the subtraction operation is entered. In contrast the

---

[38] http://www.nist.gov/public_affairs/releases/n02-10.htm; U.S. Department of Commerce's National Institute of Standards and Technology (NIST), the bugs and glitches cost the U.S. economy about $59.5 billion a year. – June 28, 2002

[39] The "-"at the beginning of the method name indicates where I added trace to get this coverage.

94

same functionality of entering "-3.14159" in the COSA Trace Table 8.1 below is accomplished between trace sequence 1 through to 10 where the same subtraction operation has been entered. There are 35 steps for ITE versus ten steps for COSA.

#	State	e→sig	Val	#	State	e→sig	Val	#	State	e→sig	Val
1	-calc	0		37	-frac1	2	-3.	73	-frac2	0	-2.
2	-calc	0		38	Frac1			74	-int2	0	-2.
3	-calc	1		39	-frac1	1	-3.	75	-int2	3	-2.
4	-ready	0		40	-frac1	1010	-3.	76	-frac2	2	-2.
5	-ready	2		41	-frac1	1010	-3.1	77	Frac2		
6	ready			42	-frac1	1010	-3.14	78	-frac2	1	-2.
7	-ready	1		43	-frac1	1010	-3.141	79	-frac2	1010	-2.
8	-begin	0		44	-frac1	1010	-3.1415	80	-frac2	1010	-2.1
9	-begin	2		45	-frac1	1107	-3.14159	81	-frac2	1010	-2.14
10	begin			46	-Oper1	1107	-3.14159	82	-frac2	1010	-2.141
11	**-begin**	**1**		47	**-frac1**	**3**	**-3.14159**	83	**-frac2**	**1010**	**-2.1415**
12	**-begin**	**1107**		48	-opEnt	0	-3.14159	84	-frac2	1102	-2.14159
13	**-negate1**	**0,**	**0**	49	-Oper1	0	-3.14159	85	-Oper2	1102	-2.14159
14	**-begin,**	**0**		50	-Oper1	3	-3.14159	86	-frac2	3	-2.14159
15	**-calc,**	**0**		51	-opEnt	2	-3.14159	87	**-result**	**0**	**-2.14159**
16	-begin,	3		52	opEnt			88	-Oper2	0	-2.14159
17	-ready	3		53	-opEnt	1	-3.14159	89	-ready	0	-2.14159
18	-ready	0		54	-opEnt	1107	-3.14159	90	-calc	0	-2.14159
19	**-negate1**	**2**	**0**	55	-negate2	0	0	91	-Oper2	3	-2.14159
20	negate1			56	-opEnt	0	0	92	-ready	2	-2.14159
21	**-negate1**	**1**	**-0**	57	-opEnt	3	0	93	ready		-2.14159
22	**-negate1**	**1010**	**-0**	58	-negate2	2	0	94	-result	2	-2.14159
23	-int1	0	-3	59	negate2			95	result		-2.14159
24	**-negate1**	**0**	**-3**	60	-negate2	1	-0	96	-eval	1104	-2.14159
25	-Oper1	0	-3	61	-negate2	1010	-0	97	-result	1	-1
26	-calc	0		62	-int2	0	-2	98	-result	100	-1
27	**-negate1**	**3**	**-3**	63	-negate2	0	-2	99	-ready	100	-1
28	-Oper1	2	-3	64	-Oper2	0	-2	100	-calc	100	-1
29	Oper1			65	-calc	0		101	-result	3	-1
30	-int1	2	-3	66	-negate2	3	-2	102	ready	3	-1
31	int1			67	-Oper2	2	-2	103	final	0	-1
32	-int1	1	-3	68	Oper2			104	calc	0	-1
33	-int1	1101	-3	69	-int2	2	-2	105	calc	3	-1
34	-frac1	0	-3.	70	int2			106	final	2	-1
35	-int1	0	-3.	71	-int2	1	-2	107	final	1	-1
36	-int1	3	-3.	72	-int2	1101	-2				

Table 8.0
ITE Calculator Trace

Starting in the ITE trace at 48 the subtraction operation is entered. To understand what was going on in the ITE approach the logic in the routines must be examined.

To handle the first operand there are eight "switch" statements, 33 "case" statements, and three "if" statements. The following shows the routine name followed by the number of "case" statements followed by the number of "if" statements:

procedure	"case"	"if"
"calc"	4	0
"ready"	6	0
"begin"	2	2
"negated1"	5	0
"int1"	4	0
"operand1"	3	0
"frac1"	4	0
"opentered"	5	1

For the subtraction operation there are three switch statements, thirteen case statements, and one if statement. The routines from trace 48 to trace 59 are:

procedure	"case"	"if"
"opentered"	5	1
"operand1"	3	0
"negated2"	5	0

At trace 59 the negation of the second operand is recognized. From trace 62 through to trace 90 where the "calc" routine is recognized and a result is created. The routines include:

procedure	"case"	"if"
"negated2"	5	0
"int2"	4	0
"operand2"	4	0
"calc"	4	0
"frac2"	3	0
"result"	1	0
"ready"	6	0

In the final result section there are seven "switch" statements, 27 "case" statements, and one "if" statement. The final result is produced at trace 97 and the application "unwinds" through trace 107.

That was a lot of logic to go through, but it truly illustrates the complexity of the ITE approach. With no temporal component, the ITE application must redundantly test to determine where it's executing because the application really doesn't know.

Count	Step	Trace	Eng	Dynamic	Static	Action	Value
1	+T= 0;	100	Off;	44;	44;	Negate;	N= -
2	+T= 1;	101	Off;	1;	1;	Any_Number;	N= -3
3	–F= 1;	101	On;	59;	1;	Ignore;	N=
4	+T= 2;	102	Off;	59;	59;	One_Period;	N= -3.
5	+T= 3;	103	Off;	1;	1;	Any_Number;	N= -3.1
6	+T= 3;	103	Off;	1;	1;	Any_Number;	N= -3.14
7	+T= 3;	103	Off;	1;	1;	Any_Number;	N= -3.141
8	+T= 3;	103	Off;	1;	1;	Any_Number;	N= -3.1415
9	+T= 3;	103	Off;	1;	1;	Any_Number;	N= -3.14159
10	–F= 3;	103	On;	44;	1;	Ignore;	N=
11	–F= 4;	104	On;	44;	12;	Ignore;	N=
12	–F= 5;	105	On;	44;	11;	Ignore;	N=
13	–F= 6;	106	On;	44;	1;	Push_Disp;	N=
14	–F= 7;	500	On;	44;	43;	Ignore;	N=
15	+T= 8;	501	On;	1;	44;	Subtraction;	N= -3.14159
16	+T= 12;	700	Off;	1;	1;	Engine_Off;	N= -3.14159
17	+T= 13;	701	Off;	44;	44;	Negate;	N= -
18	+T= 14;	702	Off;	1;	1;	Any_Number;	N= -2
19	–F= 14;	702	Off;	59;	1;	Ignore;	N=
20	+T= 15;	703	Off;	59;	59;	One_Period;	N= -2.
21	+T= 16;	704	Off;	1;	1;	Any_Number;	N= -2.1
22	+T= 16;	704	Off;	1;	1;	Any_Number;	N= -2.14
23	+T= 16;	704	Off;	1;	1;	Any_Number;	N= -2.141
24	+T= 16;	704	Off;	1;	1;	Any_Number;	N= -2.1415
25	+T= 16;	704	Off;	1;	1;	Any_Number;	N= -2.14159
26	–F= 16;	705	On;	13;	1;	Ignore;	N=
27	–F= 18;	706	On;	13;	12;	Ignore;	N=
28	–F= 17;	707	On;	13;	1;	Save_Disp;	N=
29	–F= 19;	900	On;	13;	11;	Ignore;	N=
30	+T= 20;	901	Off;	13;	13;	Equals;	N= -1

Trace 8.1
COSA Calculator Trace

Temporal COSA knows exactly where it is at all times. The only testing required by COSA is a match between the dynamic state coming into the engine from an event and the static state that is predicted to be correct based on the a piori knowledge of the

Extended BNF Table design. The correct prediction is based on a temporal understanding of the logic that has been analyzed and designed into the COSA Extended BNF Table.

Examining more comparisons between the traditional ITE approach and COSA shows that the ITE calculator example written in C++ uses 112 "if" / "case" statements, has 577 lines of code in the logic, 694 lines of code in support of the logic, and 373 lines of code in the include files, for a total of 1,644 lines of code and has an overall complexity[40] of 195. The only caveat to this example is that Samek is introducing a "Quantum" architecture to state machines, which introduces some overhead.

The COSA calculator example uses one "if" / "case" statement, has 553 lines of code using Borland's v7.0 Delphi Environment and has an overall complexity of 57. When the COSA calculator was implemented in C++ (Microsoft .NET 2003 Developer Studio), it had 527 lines of code. The difference in size and complexity is a result of the COSA engineered software strategy where the engine is in temporal control and an orthogonal implementation is used for control-flow and data-flow.

The ITE spatial calculator used in this example was thoroughly designed, discussed, and published[41] as an example in another book. According to the SEI PowerPoint presentation[42], designed applications are smaller than if they hadn't been designed. The point here is that design is important, but architecture is critical. A temporal architecture like COSA makes a difference in the size of an application.

---

[40] CDOC Documentation Tool for C, C++ and Java, www.swbs.com and www.softwareblacksmiths.com using feature called CCALL™ caller/called hierarchy ("flow structure") between functions.
[41] Samek, Miro, PhD, *Practical Statecharts in C/C++*, CMP Books, © 2002.
[42] "PSP II-Designing and Verifying State Machines," Carnegie Mellon – Software Engineering Institute, February 2005, Slide Number 5.

The following two columns compare the ITE procedures to the COSA procedures used in building the simple numbers in the calculator example.

ITE Approach	COSA Approach
23 lines of code in "negated1" 5 case statements	5 lines of code in "Negate"
23 lines of code in "negated2" 5 case statements	5 lines of code in "Any_Number"
17 lines of code in "operand1" 3 case statements	11 lines of code "save_disp"
22 lines of code in "operand2" 4 case statements	11 lines of code "push_disp"
16 lines of code in "zero1" 3 case statements	
16 lines of code in "zero2" 3 case statements	
16 lines of code in "int1" 4 case statements	
16 lines of code in "int2" 4 case statements	
12 lines of code in "frac1" 3 case statements	5 lines of code in "One_Period"
12 lines of code in "frac2" 3 case statements	
29 lines of code in "opEntered" 5 case statements	

The number of "case" statements in an application indicates how state is understood in the ITE approach. The equivalent procedures in the COSA approach are only concerned about data manipulation; these procedures have nothing to do with logic.

Finding Reuse in ITE vs. COSA

The ability to find a way to reuse routines and logic is hampered by the intertwining logic and data manipulation in the ITE approach. Resulting in the logic design in the ITE approach having to create nearly duplicate routines "int1" and "int2", "negate1" and "negate2", "frac1" and "frac2", and "operand1" and "operand2".

When a developer is looking for routines to reuse, the spaghetti code approach of ITE in Figure 8.2 as compared to the simple flow of Figure 8.3, makes the choice easy. In order to reuse logic, routines, or components they must be easily understood. Generally speaking when a developer is looking for software to reuse it must have been well documented and fully understood. Most ITE software does not fall under that definition. Therefore the developer must analyze the prospective reuse software for suitability. When analyzing COSA for reuse the specification, BNF Tree, Extended BNF Table, and procedures are all available and very simple. This makes COSA the best choice for reuse.

For a better understanding about reuse compare these two applications, side-by-side, with trace added. More than any other indicator, adding trace shows the difference between the traditional spatial approach and the temporal COSA approach. With COSA it's a matter of adding two lines of code to enable the two trace methods. Adding trace in the COSA application is easy. But when the same coverage of trace is added to the traditional approach it takes a significant amount of work. In this case it takes 15 lines of code spread throughout the application, increasing the chances of error. COSA produces simpler code, which is easier to develop, maintain and reuse.

A Note on Static and Dynamic Trace

When ITE logic is scaled to large applications changes are extremely difficult to trace for change control documentation. Figure 8.3 is an application of about one thousand lines of code. Imagine what the call diagram looks like for larger applications with a million lines of code. Now add the ability through polymorphism and other mechanisms to dynamically change an application. The logic of ITE becomes even more complex. As a result the logic becomes even more difficult to statically and dynamically trace.

An Ad Hoc Calculator

The previous comparisons between ITE and COSA are based on the architectural framework each espouses. For an additional comparison an Ad Hoc ITE five-function calculator is created. Delphi was used because of its ability to rapidly create the prototype.

The creation of the four-function portion of the calculator was relatively easy. Saving the actual operation (for instance plus) until after the equal sign is clicked requires saving an operator state.

At this stage of its development the ad hoc approach looks clean. As other parts of the specifications are added the problem becomes more difficult. The negate function is now added using the subtract operator (remember no change sign key). With ITE this requires testing every section to see if the calculator is pre-operand or post-operate. Changing one piece of the logic requires all pieces to be reexamined.

At this point the code is "patchy" because of the additional state testing required to add the negate specification. However, when the multiplication of two negative numbers is tested the calculator fails. Code has to be added to handle negating the first operand differently from the second operand. The negation of the first operand occurs before a digit is entered. After the logic determines a number is not entered it must determine what happens next, operator or sign. The negation of the second operand occurs after the operator has been entered but before a digit is entered. The law of unintended consequences holds true. Once the multiply works the subtraction has to be re-coded.

Next the percent function is added. Again, it is like adding a "patch" to a "patch" resulting in the additional testing of the code that was originally created to perform a different function. Once the percent is working the chain operation is tried and the calculator fails. The law of unintended consequences continues to hold true. Regression testing is starting to take on a life of its own.

The ITE Ad Hoc design now requires additional states to be added into working code to perform some additional function for which the original code was not intended. This next "patch" has to determine if there is a pending operation with a first and second operation. State must be saved to allow for the completion of the operation or allow for the continuation of other operations. Somehow, this logic gets "fitted" into the existing logic without breaking what is working. This is a "patch" on a "patch" on a "patch", the essence of the problems with spatial software development. AND, the law of unintended consequences continues to hold true because of this spatial approach.

Summary

In examining the flow analysis of the procedure calls of COSA and traditional ITE it can be seen that ITE is substantially more complex. When trace is used the comparison continues to illustrate the simplicity of coding in COSA.

COSA results in a highly predictable engineered approach to software. It's implemented as a state machine with a time component, inherent trace, robustness, and temporal logic reduces the complexity of software development. Adding logic or changing the way data is manipulated in COSA minimizes the law of unintended consequences.

Even a simple Ad Hoc calculator demonstrates how difficult it is to create clean logic with an ITE approach. The ad hoc calculator discussion in this chapter provides a good basis for understanding why software is difficult to implement and by comparison why COSA is truly revolutionary.

With the ITE approach to software, testing is extremely difficult because it is equally difficult to place any kind of metrics in the software. One of the problems in comparing the ITE approach to the power of COSA, is in providing the metrics in a way that is equal and complete. The Department of Commerce report produced by NIST[43] points out that software testing is just plain inadequate. The inherent structure of COSA significantly reduces the problems of software testing. The trace and structure lend access to automated tools able to analyze the application's structure from specification to final product resulting in a *COSA certification*.

---

[43] Gregory Tassey, "The Economic Impacts of Inadequate Infrastructure for Software Testing", May 2002, National Institute of Standards and Technology.

9

Chapter 9 – COSA Comment Parser Example

This chapter takes a look at the logic in the C and C++ comment parser and finds some unexpected results. The comment parser logic is interesting because it demonstrates the power in ordering the logic of temporal states and is small enough to be covered adequately in this book.

There are two forms of C++ comment. The traditional C comment starts anywhere in a line of text with a "slash star" and ending with a "star slash". This form of comment can include multiple lines as long as the last line in the comment ends with a "star slash". The newer form of single line C++ comment is to place a "slash slash" anywhere on a line followed by any character up to the end of line.

Valid comments are in bold as follows, that "*slash star until star slash*" on the line is not a valid comment because it is inside a valid "slash slash" comment and should be ignored by the parser. Likewise the "//" inside the second comment should be ignored.

> "Valid code /_* / not yet // **now we have a comment /* until */ the end of line.**"
> "/* ← **starts, not → // also a valid comment // including**
> **Continuing the next line // */** ← first ends, new starts // **new comment.**"

Any parser should ignore embedded comments with a minimal amount of wasted state analysis. The following two productions will handle all "C++" type comments.

Cmnt = <any>* <iDiv47> <iMul42> <any>* <iMul42> <iDiv47> <any>* |
<any>* <iDiv47> <iDiv47> <any>* <eol>;
BNF 9.0

The <any> means any character or sequence of characters except a slash. The
true/false actions can now be added to each state as they have been defined in a vertical
tree.

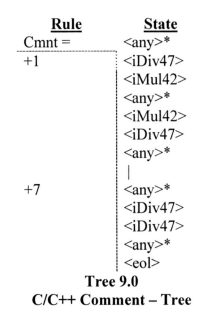

Rule	State
Cmnt =	<any>*
+1	<iDiv47>
	<iMul42>
	<any>*
	<iMul42>
	<iDiv47>
	<any>*
	|
+7	<any>*
	<iDiv47>
	<iDiv47>
	<any>*
	<eol>

Tree 9.0
C/C++ Comment – Tree

Most of the action in parsing comments is to ignore what's going on. "Cmnt" starts
the tradition "C" comment parsing and "Cmnt+7" starts the new "C++" comment
parsing. When any character but a "slash" is encountered the true action is to turn off the
engine and get another character. If the <any> state is false then a "slash" has been found
and the proper action is to move to the next temporal state at "Cmnt+1" to verify the
"slash". If the next character is a "star" then the "C" comment has started. If the
character is not a "star" then the transition is to "Cmnt+9" to see if the character is a

second "slash" starting a single line "C++" comment. If neither type of comment is started control is returned to the "Cmnt" looking for any character but a "slash". "EngOff" is the action and means do nothing and move on to the next character. The "StartCmt" is the beginning of a comment and the "EndCmt" is the end of a comment. The "Ignore" is a temporal placeholder.

Step	State	True	Next	False	Next	Trace
Cmnt =	<any>*	EngOff	Cmnt	Ignore	Cmnt+1	100
+1	<iDiv47>	Ignore	Cmnt+2	EngOff	Cmnt	101
+2	<iMul42>	StartCmt	Cmnt+3	Ignore	Cmnt+9	102
+3	<any>*	EngOff	Cmnt+3	Ignore	Cmnt+4	103
+4	<iMul42>	Star	Cmnt+3	EngOff	Cmnt+5	104
+5	<iDiv47>	EndCmt	Cmnt	EngOff	Cmnt+3	105
+6	**<any>***	**EngOff**	**Cmnt**	**Ignore**	**Cmnt**	**106**
+7	<any>*	EngOff	Cmnt	Ignore	Cmnt	200
+8	<iDiv47>	Ignore	Cmnt+9	EngOff	Cmnt	201
+9	<iDiv47>	StartCmt	Cmnt+10	EngOff	Cmnt	202
+10	<any>*	EngOff	Cmnt+11	EngOff	Cmnt+11	203
+11	<eol>	EndCmt	Cmnt	EngOff	Cmnt+11	204

Table 9.0
C/C++ Comment – COSA Extended BNF

In general the line at Trace 100 is an application doing some work related to other activities. Only when a "slash" is detected does the application need to perform some other specific action like to determine if this is the beginning of a comment. When a comment doesn't start the application must still deal with the "slash" that was found. It does that by returning control to the application at Trace 100. In essence the comment determination required a look-ahead character. The routine "StartCmt" is comparing the look-ahead character to the static state. When the comparison is true the comment begins. When the comparison is false control is returned to the application.

In analyzing the logic to determine where reductions can be made it is determined that the "star slash" is not the same as "slash star" therefore; the commutative law won't apply as a way of reducing logic because order is everything in the *temporal* world. Some form of the associative and distributive laws may apply.

Action Reduction

If a production begins and ends with the same element, and the temporal behavior returns control to the first element, then ONE of the elements is redundant.

Reduction 1:

The step at "Cmnt+6" in the Table 9.0 marked in bold isn't used in finding comment logic; further the same behavior is available within the logic in the right temporal sequence. In the first production in BNF 9.1, the bold <any>* element at the end of the production is redundant with the first <any>* element.

Cmnt =   <any>* <iDiv47> <iMul42> <any>* <iMul42> <iDiv47> **<any>***
           | <any>* <iDiv47> <iDiv47><any>* <eol>;
BNF 9.1
Before Reduction

Considering the temporal component: when the last <slash> in the first production is found, control will return to the first <any>* element[44]. Both of the "Next" temporal steps return control to the beginning of the comment logic, therefore, the row "Cmnt+6" and the bold <any>* can be removed. The action reduction results in the two productions in BNF 9.2.

Cmnt =   <any>* <iDiv47> <iMul42> <any>* <iMul42> <iDiv47> |
              <any>* <iDiv47> <iDiv47> <any>* <eol>;
BNF 9.2

After Reduction

Reduction 2:

The next step is to determine what the actions do. The parsing of C++ comments is a temporal logic problem. The actions don't have any function other than to get the next character through turning the engine off. The <any>* character is the same as ignoring or not ignoring a <iDiv47>. The first <any>* can be removed (in the sense that this is another part of the application) and the parser receives characters comparing them to the <iDiv47> until a true match occurs. After detecting a <iDiv47> <iMul42> the parser is looking for the occurrence of a <iMul42>. The second <any>* character is the same as ignoring or not ignoring a <iMul42>. Removing the second <any>* character the parser receives characters looking for a <iMul42> until a true match occurs.

The second production is for the C++ "slash slash" comment. The two <any>* characters follow the same logic which allows the two <any>* characters to be removed resulting in seven steps in BNF 9.3.

Cmnt =   **<any>*** <iDiv47> < iMul42> **<any>*** <iMul42> <iDiv47> |
                     <any>* <iDiv47> <iDiv47> **<any>*** <eol>;
                               Before Reduction

Cmnt =   <iDiv47> <iMul42> <iMul42> <iDiv47> |
                     <iDiv47> <iDiv47> <eol>;
                               BNF 9.3
                            After Reduction

Action Coalescence

By aligning the productions, common elements can be found. Both productions key on the <slash> to begin a comment.

*If a production shares a sequence of common elements, the subordinate production can be reduced by the sequence of common elements it shares **one time.** The proper temporal connections must be made. The connection is made between the element that is subsequent the remaining common element and the element subsequent to the removed common element.*

Reduction 3:

The first <iDiv47> in the first production is shared by the first <iDiv47> in the subordinate production. Therefore, the subordinate <iDiv47> can be removed from the second production. The new subordinate production starts with a <iDiv47> but the one time reduction has been used.

Comment = **<iDiv47> <iMul42> <iMul42> <iDiv47> |**
<iDiv47> <iDiv47> <eol>;
BNF 9.4
Before Reduction

With Action Coalescence there must be a temporal consideration. When the first <iDiv47> in the second production is removed there needs to be a connection between the second element in the first production and the new first element in the second production. The connection is from the <iMul42> on a *false* action to the <iDiv47>. Keeping the elements in the proper temporal frame, the second production is coalesced with the first production to eliminate the pipe resulting in a single production. That was a lot of logic and here is what it looks like in the BNF with the false temporal line followed by the Extended BNF Rules Table.

Comment = (<iDiv47> <iMul42> < iMul42> <iDiv47>) (<iDiv47> <eol>);
BNF 9.5
After Reduction

With the BNF reduced from the original twelve elements to its current form of six elements. The trace numbers are no longer sequential, only some of the original trace numbers from Table 9.0 are reflected in the new Table 9.1.

Step	State	True	Next	False	Next	Trace
Cmnt	<iDiv47>	Slash	Cmnt+1	EngOff	Cmnt	100
+1	<iMul42>	StartCmt	Cmnt+2	Ignore	Cmnt+4	102
+2	<iMul42>	Star	Cmnt+3	EngOff	Cmnt+2	104
+3	<iDiv47>	EndCmt	Cmnt	EngOff	Cmnt+2	105
+4	<iDiv47>	**StartCmt**	Cmnt+5	EngOff	Cmnt	202
+5	<eol>	EndCmt	Cmnt	EngOff	Cmnt+5	204

Table 9.1
C/C++ First Logic Comment – COSA Extended BNF

First Temporal Logic

When COSA is implemented in a tool, the logic is easier to follow because of the animation. For this book the logic is: if the parser gets a "slash slash" then the transition is from step "Cmnt" as true to "Cmnt+1" as false to "Cmnt+4" as true to "Cmnt+5" where the parser searches for an end of line (EOL), whereupon temporal control is returned to step "Cmnt". If a character is not a "slash", then the engine is turned off and the next character is fetched. The behaviors "Slash", "StartCmt", "Star", and "EndCmt" all turn off the engine to allow the parser to fetch the next character.

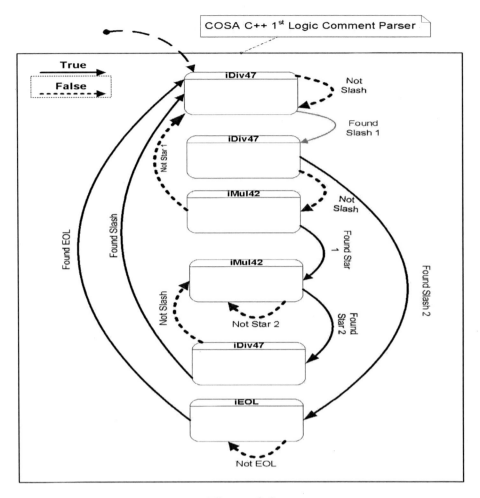

Figure 9.0
C/C++ First Logic Comment – Statechart

If the parser gets a "slash star" then the transitions are from "Cmnt" to "Cmnt+1" to "Cmnt+2" where the scan remains until a "star" is found followed by a "slash." When the terminal element is found control returns to "Cmnt."

By the logic in table 9.1 the "slash star star slash" process takes four steps. Four steps are needed to accommodate the "slash slash eol" process. The combined count is eight steps.

111

Second Temporal Logic

There is another way to arrange the logic. Herein lies the artistry of temporal engineering – and might lead to other understandings about temporal logic. By reconsidering the order of the steps the logic can be optimized. Gains or loses in performance tuning can be determined by counting the state transitions. When the "slash slash" is at the beginning of the logic it takes three steps to conclude a comment. The "slash star star slash" logic now requires five steps making a total of eight steps for both comment processes. However, this rearranging significantly reduces the number of steps needed in an application if the "slash slash" comment is used the most.

Comment =   <iDiv47> <iDiv47> <iMul42> <iMul42> <iDiv47> <eol>;
BNF 9.6

Step	State	True	Next	False	Next	Trace
Cmnt	<iDiv47>	Slash	Cmnt+1	EngOff	Cmnt	101
+1	<iDiv47>	**StartCmt**	**Cmnt+5**	Ignore	Cmnt+2	**202**
+2	<iMul42>	StartCmt	Cmnt+3	EngOff	Cmnt	102
+3	<iMul42>	Star	Cmnt+4	EngOff	Cmnt+3	104
+4	<iDiv47>	EndCmt	Cmnt	EngOff	Cmnt+3	105
+5	<eol>	EndCmt	Cmnt	EngOff	Cmnt+5	204

Table 9.2
C/C++ Second Logic Comment – COSA Extended BNF

The new logic goes like this: if the parser gets a "slash slash" then the transition is from step "Cmnt" to "Cmnt+1" to "Cmnt+5" where the parser waits for an end of line (EOL), whereupon temporal control is returned to step "Cmnt". If the character is not a "slash", then the engine is turned off and the next character is fetched. The behaviors "Slash", "StartCmt", "Star", "EndCmt" and "EngOff" all turn off the engine to allow the parser to fetch the next character.

112

The next comment type, "slash star", causes the engine to transition from step "Cmnt" to "Cmnt+1" on a false state, then the engine transitions to "Cmnt+2" with a true state. The engine on the next character transitions to "Cmnt+3" where the engine continues processing waiting for the next comment "star" to trigger. The comment will only terminate when the "star slash" sequence is found. At that point the temporal control is returned to step "Cmnt".

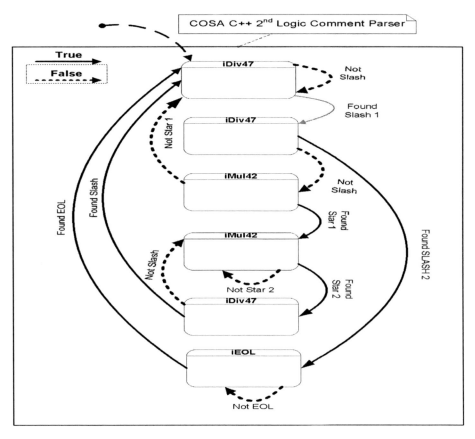

Figure 9.1
C/C++ Second Logic Comment – Statechart

The logic in Table 9.0 has been reduced from twelve steps to six steps in Table 9.2. The duplicate "slash slash" and "star star" can't be replaced because they each have different temporal behaviors.

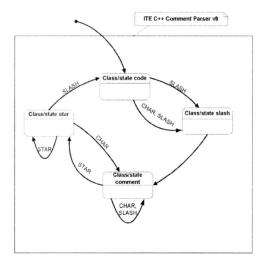

Figure 9.2a
Original ITE C *Only* – Comment Parser Statechart

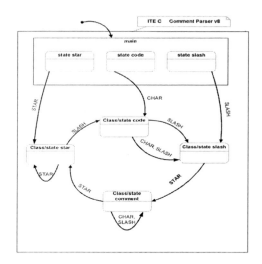

Figure 9.2b
ITE C *Only* – Comment Parser Statechart

Visio was used to create the state diagrams in Figure 9.2 (a and b). Figure 9.2a is the representation that the traditional ITE approach uses for the states in version 8 of the C comment parser. Figure 9.2b is a complete representation of the application including the states Samek[45] refers to in the file "Cparser8.c", which uses a "switch" and three "case" statements to test for "/", "*", and default. Each state box is also a class in this implementation of his framework. The ITE "cparser8" implementation uses five "switch" statements with a total of 13 "case" conditions shown in Figure 9.2b. Using this many "switch/case" statements is a strong indication of a spatial implementation. This non-temporal approach must repeatedly retest to determine where it is in its logic sequence.

Unlike other implementations, COSA doesn't need to keep track of any states for this application. What is normally thought of in state machines is (in COSA) a new facet based on temporal transitions. Instead of actions constantly checking on variables that were set as states, the logic dominates and the conditions are considered in a temporal manner. (This could be called a time machine but the notion has been abused by decades of science fiction.)

Testing the Comment Logic

On a CD that came with Samek's book there is a test file for the comment parser. According to the word count function in Microsoft Word, the "test.c" file has 52 characters (including spaces), on three lines. Eighteen of the characters in the test file are part of a valid comment; one "/" is not part of a valid comment. That leaves 33 characters plus the three-newline terminators that needed to be ignored →

(19 + 33 + 3 = 55).

The Provided Test File:

```
/* test */
case '/': /* / */ SIG; break;
/* the end */
```

[45] Samek, Miro, PhD, *Practical Statecharts in C/C++*, CMP Books, © 2002.

COSA Execution Analysis

The right list box of this screenshot (Figure 9.3) shows the C++ comment trace. The step count is the first column. The second column is the state true or false. The number is the trace value followed by the character from the file being parsed.

The first character in the file is a "slash", so the first state is true in Table 9.4. The transition to the second line is false to trace 202 since the next character is not a "slash." The parser engine continues and finds the "star" at trace 102, where it churns away on the text. At step 10 the trace at 104, the parser engine finds a true "star" taking in nine characters. At step 11, the trace at 104 is true, and at trace 105 the comment concludes to the end of line at trace 100. That's 90.9% efficient, checking ten characters toward the desired work done in 11 states. At step 19, a true trace 100 is found, but it is <u>not</u> a comment beginning, so at step 22, the parser engine is back on the hunt for comments. At steps 24 and 26, the engine has found the beginning of the next comment. A "slash" is fount but it is internal to the comment at step 28 at trace 104 where the logic is looking for the second "star."

//
// Static
// Rules
	State	True
		Action
			Next
			True
			Rule
				False
				Action
					Next
					False
					Rule
						Trace

(rCmnt,	iDiv47,	Slash,	rCmnt+1,	EngOff,	rCmnt,	100);
(rCmnt+1,	iDiv47,	StartCmt,	rCmnt+5,	Ignore,	rCmnt+2,	202);
(rCmnt+2,	iMul42,	StartCmt	rCmnt+3,	EngOff,	rCmnt,	102);
(rCmnt+3,	iMul42,	Star,	rCmnt+4,	EngOff,	rCmnt+3,	104);
(rCmnt+4,	iDiv47,	EndCmt,	rCmnt,	EngOff,	rCmnt+3,	105);
(rCmnt+5,	iEOL,	EndCmt,	rCmnt,	EngOff,	rCmnt+5,	204);

Table 9.4
COSA Extended BNF Rules – Second Logic

```
┌─────────────────────────────────────────────────────────────┐
│ 7ℰ COSA C / C++ Comment Parser                    _ □ X      │
├─────────────────────────────────────────────────────────────┤
│ File  Run  About                                             │
│ ┌───────────────────────────┐ ┌──────────────────────────┐ │
│ │ First Temporal Logic.     │ │ found - Slash         ▲  │ │
│ │  found - Slash            │ │ 1; True- 100- /          │ │
│ │  start - Slash-Star comment│ │ 2; False- 202- *         │ │
│ │    found - Star           │ │  start - Slash-Star comment│ │
│ │      End Star-Slash comment│ │ 3; True- 102- *          │ │
│ │  found - Slash            │ │ 4; False- 104-           │ │
│ │  found - Slash            │ │ 5; False- 104- t         │ │
│ │  start - Slash-Star comment│ │ 6; False- 104- e         │ │
│ │    found - Star           │ │ 7; False- 104- s         │ │
│ │      End Star-Slash comment│ │ 8; False- 104- t         │ │
│ │  found - Slash            │ │ 9; False- 104-           │ │
│ │  start - Slash-Star comment│ │  found - Star            │ │
│ │    found - Star           │ │ 10; True- 104- *         │ │
│ │      End Star-Slash comment│ │    End Star-Slash comment│ │
│ │      End of File!         │ │ 11; True- 105- /         │ │
│ │                           │ │ 12; False- 100-          │ │
│ │                           │ │ 13; False- 100- c        │ │
│ │                           │ │ 14; False- 100- a        │ │
│ │                           │ │ 15; False- 100- s        │ │
│ │                           │ │ 16; False- 100- e        │ │
│ │                           │ │ 17; False- 100-          │ │
│ │                           │ │ 18; False- 100- '        │ │
│ │                           │ │  found - Slash           │ │
│ │                           │ │ 19; True- 100- /         │ │
│ │                           │ │ 20; False- 202- '        │ │
│ │                           │ │ 21; False- 102- '        │ │
│ │                           │ │ 22; False- 100- :        │ │
│ │                           │ │ 23; False- 100-          │ │
│ │                           │ │  found - Slash           │ │
│ │                           │ │ 24; True- 100- /         │ │
│ │                           │ │ 25; False- 202- *        │ │
│ │                           │ │  start - Slash-Star comment│ │
│ │                           │ │ 26; True- 102- *         │ │
│ │                           │ │ 27; False- 104-          │ │
│ │                           │ │ 28; False- 104- /        │ │
│ │                           │ │ 29; False- 104-          │ │
│ │                           │ │  found - Star            │ │
│ │                           │ │ 30; True- 104- *      ▼  │ │
│ └───────────────────────────┘ └──────────────────────────┘ │
└─────────────────────────────────────────────────────────────┘
```

Figure 9.3
Second Temporal Logic – Application Trace

An important point to notice about steps 27, 28, and 29 is that the engine has parsed through a "slash", and it is ignored. A "slash" means nothing at this point in "**time**" to the comment rule because the only character that will begin the end of this comment is a "star" followed by a "slash".

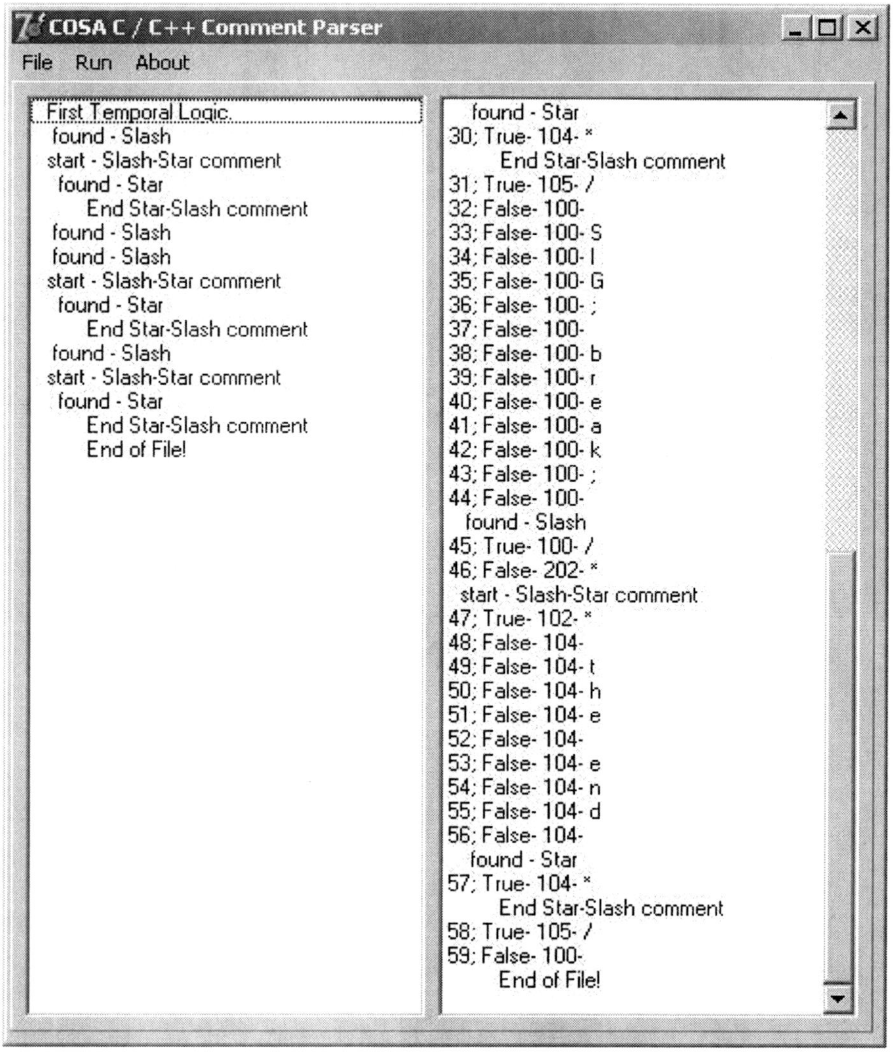

Figure 9.4
Second Temporal Logic – Application Trace

At step 30 in Figure 9.4, the parser engine has found a "star", and a "slash" at step 31 marking the end of a comment. At step 32 the parser engine is back on the hunt for a "slash" marking the beginning of the next comment. Steps 32 through 44 on this page are non-comment characters and are ignored according to the comment rules.

At step 45, the parser engine has found a "slash" and at 46 the "star" is found marking the beginning of a comment. Steps 48 through 56 are in the comment and are ignored. The end of the comment starts at step 57 and is completed at step 58. At step 59, the end of the file has been found and the application terminates. This is 93.2% efficient using the 55 total characters divided by the 59 states transitioned to the end of file.

Notice that a true trace at 202 never shows up. That is because this test file did not have a "slash slash" comment whose rule is true at trace 202. The true trace 202 would transfer the logic to rule "Cmnt+5" trace 204, to churn through characters until the end of line is reached. The ITE state diagram in Figure 9.2 doesn't include the C++ comment "//" logic but the COSA state diagram in Figure 9.0 and Figure 9.1 includes handling this option.

1; True- 100- /	21; False- 102- '	41; False- 100- a
2; False- 202- *	22; False- 100- :	42; False- 100- k
3; True- 102- *	23; False- 100-	43; False- 100- ;
4; False- 104-	24; True- 100- /	44; False- 100- <NL>
5; False- 104- t	**25; False- 202- ***	45; True- 100- /
6; False- 104- e	26; True- 102- *	**46; False- 202- ***
7; False- 104- s	27; False- 104-	47; True- 102- *
8; False- 104- t	28; False- 104- /	48; False- 104-
9; False- 104-	29; False- 104-	49; False- 104- t
10; True- 104- *	30; True- 104- *	50; False- 104- h
11; True- 105- /	31; True- 105- /	51; False- 104- e
12; False- 100- <NL>	32; False- 100-	52; False- 104-
13; False- 100- c	33; False- 100- S	53; False- 104- e
14; False- 100- a	34; False- 100- I	54; False- 104- n
15; False- 100- s	35; False- 100- G	55; False- 104- d
16; False- 100- e	36; False- 100- ;	56; False- 104-
17; False- 100-	37; False- 100-	57; True- 104- *
18; False- 100- '	38; False- 100- b	58; True- 105- /
19; True- 100- /	39; False- 100- r	59; False-100- <NL>
20; False- 202- '	40; False- 100- e	

Trace 9.0
Second Temporal Logic – Trace Output

The COSA trace file above shows the step number, the engine state, the trace number, and the character. At step 12, step 44, and step 59 are three carriage-return characters.

Traditional ITE Execution Analysis

In the ITE approach implemented by Samek there are a total of 87 transitions to cover the "test.c" file. In order to get the "Cparser8" Trace 9.1, I needed to add three "printf" lines of code to the main cpp routine. I also needed to add ten lines of "printf" to the "Cparser8" parser. That was one "printf" for each case statement. The "Cparser8.exe" is a command line MS-DOS application with the name of the test file required.

Trace 9.1 contains the trace that was added to the original "Cparser8". There are two files in "Cparser8": "Cparser8.cpp" and "Test8.cpp". "Test8" contains the Main trace where the "Switch/Case" is testing for slash, star, or any character. Between line 1 and line 4, the first comment beginning is identified. Each line represents a "Switch/Case" statement. It takes four "Switch/Case" statements to identify "/*". The only single "Switch/Case" test is the Main default when any character but a "/" or "*" is found. At line 20, the first comment is concluded. It takes 20 steps to parse the ten characters contained in "/* test */". That compares to the 11 steps taken by the Second Logic of COSA. The First Logic was tuned to the "C" style comment and only took 10 steps to process the ten characters in the comment.

```
/* test */
case '/': /* / */ SIG; break;
/* the end */
```
The Provided Test File

1 -g Main slash 2 - /
2 -g CodeState-slash 2 - /
3 -g Main star 1 - *
4 -g SlashState-Star 1 - *
5 -g Main default 0 -
6 -g CommentState-char 0 -
7 -g Main default 0 - t
8 -g CommentState-char 0 - t
9 -g Main default 0 - e
10 -g CommentState-char 0 - e
11 -g Main default 0 - s
12 -g CommentState-char 0 - s
13 -g Main default 0 - t
14 -g CommentState-char 0 - t
15 -g Main default 0 -
16 -g CommentState-char 0 -
17 -g Main star 1 - *
18 -g CommentState-star 1 - *
19 -g Main slash 2 - /
20 -g StarState-slash 2 - /
21 -g Main default 0 - <NL>
22 -g Main default 0 - c
23 -g Main default 0 - a
24 -g Main default 0 - s
25 -g Main default 0 - e
26 -g Main default 0 -
27 -g Main default 0 - '
28 -g Main slash 2 - /
29 -g CodeState-slash 2 - /
30 -g Main default 0 - '

31 -g SlashState-Char 0 - '
32 -g Main default 0 - :
33 -g Main default 0 -
34 -g Main slash 2 - /
35 -g CodeState-slash 2 - /
36 -g Main star 1 - *
37 -g SlashState-Star 1 - *
38 -g Main default 0 -
39 -g CommentState-char 0 -
40 -g Main slash 2 - /
41 -g CommentState-slash 2 - /
42 -g Main default 0 -
43 -g CommentState-char 0 -
44 -g Main star 1 - *
45 -g CommentState-star 1 - *
46 -g Main slash 2 - /
47 -g StarState-slash 2 - /
48 -g Main default 0 -
49 -g Main default 0 - S
50 -g Main default 0 - I
51 -g Main default 0 - G
52 -g Main default 0 - ;
53 -g Main default 0 -
54 -g Main default 0 - b
55 -g Main default 0 - r
56 -g Main default 0 - e
57 -g Main default 0 - a
58 -g Main default 0 - k
59 -g Main default 0 - ;
60 -g Main default 0 - <NL>

61 -g Main slash 2 - /
62 -g CodeState-slash 2 - /
63 -g Main star 1 - *
64 -g SlashState-Star 1 - *
65 -g Main default 0 -
66 -g CommentState-char 0 -
67 -g Main default 0 - t
68 -g CommentState-char 0 - t
69 -g Main default 0 - h
70 -g CommentState-char 0 - h
71 -g Main default 0 - e
72 -g CommentState-char 0 - e
73 -g Main default 0 -
74 -g CommentState-char 0 -
75 -g Main default 0 - e
76 -g CommentState-char 0 - e
77 -g Main default 0 - n
78 -g CommentState-char 0 - n
79 -g Main default 0 - d
80 -g CommentState-char 0 - d
81 -g Main default 0 –
82 -g CommentState-char 0 –
83 -g Main star 1 - *
84 -g CommentState-star 1 - *
85 -g Main slash 2 - /
86 -g StarState-slash 2 - /
87 -g Main default 0 – <NL>

Trace 9.1
ITE C Comment File – Trace Output

Five steps are required to start a comment from state 1 to state 5. It takes four steps to end the comment from state 17 to state 20. At state 28, the non-comment character "slash" begins to be processed. At state 31, the parser is back on the hunt for a valid comment beginning. At 34, the main state has found a "slash." At state 38, the parser is looking for the ending of the comment. At state 39, the application acknowledges the comment state. The only trigger that should get the parser's attention is a "star" at this point. BUT, the parser comes across another "slash" at line 40. Because the parser does not have a sense of where it is temporally, the logic must check at line 41 and determine that it's looking for a "star" where this implementation will dynamically bind to "myStarState." The states at 39, 40, and 41 are wasted states internal to the comment where everything is to be ignored.

At line 42, main is again looking for a "slash", "star", or any character. At line 44, the main has found a "star", and by line 48, it has concluded the comment and is now looking for the next comment. Main remains in line 48 through 60, pulling in characters for the Switch/Case and eventually falling through on the Default statement; the character is not a "slash" or "star." The parser detects a "slash" at line 61 and detects a "star" at line 63. From line 66 to line 82, the parser is in its comment state. At line 83, the parser finds a "star", and at line 85, the parser finds that the next character is a "slash" and the comment is over. The parser ends with the end of file at line 87.

The ITE approach is 63% efficient based on the number of valid characters, 55, divided by the 87 states.

But Wait: If you order now:

Even though the "Second Temporal Logic" discussed on is much better than the ITE approach if I had used the "First Temporal Logic" ge 115 discussed earlier this would have resulted in removing the bold steps shown in Trace 9.0 at steps 2, 25, and 46. The result would be 55 total characters divided by 56 states transitioned. That is an efficiency of 98.2%.

Why wasn't the temporal logic 100% efficient? The test file had a non-comment "slash" outside of a comment block. The line consists of "case '/': /* / */ SIG; break;". The "slash" used in the "case" statement would be valid in the C language and a COSA parser would have processed the "slash". But the focus on this example was to catch C

122

style comments. COSA was distracted from steps 19 to 21 and the ITE was distracted from steps 28 to 32 by the offending "slash".

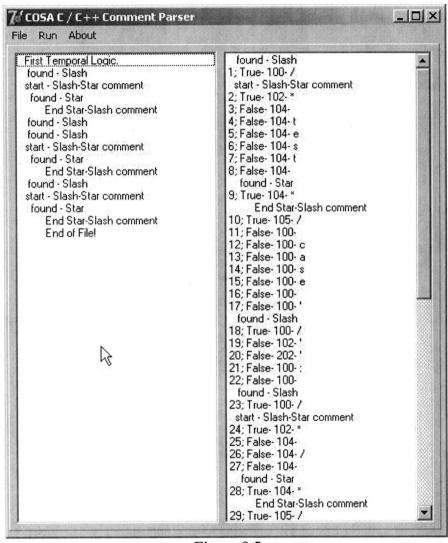

Figure 9.5
First Temporal Logic – Application Trace

In figure 9.5 all of the trace 100 are outside of a comment. All of the trace104 are inside of a comment looking for a "star" to end the comment.

The ability to performance tune pure logic can be a significant gain to embedded systems. All real-time embedded operating system were written using the standard ITE approach. These ITE applications can be found in medical devices, military devices, communication devices, toys, and games to name a few.

```
7 COSA C / C++ Comment Parser                    _ □ ×
File  Run  About

First Temporal Logic.              27; False- 104-
found - Slash                       found - Star
start - Slash-Star comment         28; True- 104- *
 found - Star                          End Star-Slash comment
  End Star-Slash comment           29; True- 105- /
found - Slash                      30; False- 100-
found - Slash                      31; False- 100- S
start - Slash-Star comment         32; False- 100- I
 found - Star                      33; False- 100- G
  End Star-Slash comment           34; False- 100- ;
found - Slash                      35; False- 100-
start - Slash-Star comment         36; False- 100- b
 found - Star                      37; False- 100- r
  End Star-Slash comment           38; False- 100- e
  End of File!                     39; False- 100- a
                                   40; False- 100- k
                                   41; False- 100- ;
                                   42; False- 100-
                                    found - Slash
                                   43; True- 100- /
                                    start - Slash-Star comment
                                   44; True- 102- *
                                   45; False- 104-
                                   46; False- 104- t
                                   47; False- 104- h
                                   48; False- 104- e
                                   49; False- 104-
                                   50; False- 104- e
                                   51; False- 104- n
                                   52; False- 104- d
                                   53; False- 104-
                                    found - Star
                                   54; True- 104- *
                                    End Star-Slash comment
                                   55; True- 105- /
                                   56; False- 100-
                                    End of File!
```

Figure 9.6
First Temporal Logic – Application Trace

The trace file output for the first temporal logic shows how efficient the COSA approach is when it is tuned to the problem.

1; True- 100- /	21; False- 100- :	41; False- 100- ;
2; True- 102- *	22; False- 100-	42; False- 100- <NL>
3; False- 104-	23; True- 100- /	43; True- 100- /
4; False- 104- t	24; True- 102- *	44; True- 102- *
5; False- 104- e	25; False- 104-	45; False- 104-
6; False- 104- s	26; False- 104- /	46; False- 104- t
7; False- 104- t	27; False- 104-	47; False- 104- h
8; False- 104-	28; True- 104- *	48; False- 104- e
9; True- 104- *	29; True- 105- /	49; False- 104-
10; True- 105- /	30; False- 100-	50; False- 104- e
11; False- 100- <NL>	31; False- 100- S	51; False- 104- n
12; False- 100- c	32; False- 100- I	52; False- 104- d
13; False- 100- a	33; False- 100- G	53; False- 104-
14; False- 100- s	34; False- 100- ;	54; True- 104- *
15; False- 100- e	35; False- 100-	55; True- 105- /
16; False- 100-	36; False- 100- b	56; False- 100- <NL>
17; False- 100- '	37; False- 100- r	
18; True- 100- /	38; False- 100- e	
19; False- 102- '	39; False- 100- a	
20; False- 202- '	40; False- 100- k	

Trace 9.2
First Temporal Logic – Trace Output

The ability to decide to detune the temporal logic in favor of one outcome over another is equally important. This temporal logic tuning is one way to differentiate between the so-called "home" system and the "professional" system. A cost differential could be justified because of the additional work involved in the tuning effort. The same differential would apply in military applications where one temporal-logic could lock onto a target more rapidly than another. The power in COSA is that the Extended BNF Table is also data. Depending on the frequency of one data structure over another being analyzed, COSA could allow the Extended BNF Table to be restructured dynamically for better performance.

Summary

This chapter continued to demonstrate how the specification remains in sync with the application. A couple of techniques were introduced for reducing logic. There was a comparison of two different logic approaches solving the same problem. Tuning the logic to one expected type of data structure showed an improvement in performance for that data structure but reduced the performance for other data flow structures.

The temporal approach to logic results in a better understanding of how an application works with less redundant code, better optimization, and smaller and faster applications. Temporal logic separate from data manipulation allows for more performance tuning. Using "Action Reduction" and "Action Coalesence" can further reduce temporal logic. This logic reduction is important when the logic is applied to business rules or process rules resulting in a direct reduction in cost.

10

Chapter 10 – The COSA Data Parser Example

Nearly every project in business needs a data parser. Data parsers are generally used to clean or filter data. They can be a part of an application attached to a database or the Internet. The Data Parser in this example will use a simple text data file. The data file has a single line record containing names and phone numbers that will be defined in detail.

The Data Parser Application has a standard GUI layout with the traditional menu File with standard Open item. This implementation uses one main and three subordinate COSA engines. The main engine "RunGUI" controls the user interaction through the menu and manages the other two engines. In addition to overall control the GUI engine adds the parser results to the GUI report tree. The "RunGUI" Extended BNF Table contains twenty-one entries.

The second subordinate engine "RunLexer" controls the scanner. The scanner manages the processing of characters returning tokens to the GUI engine. The "RunLexer" Extended BNF Table contains 128 entries.

The third subordinate engine "RunParser" receives the token form the GUI engine and determines from the rules if the structure of the data file is correct. The Parser engine then sends the results of what is found to the GUI engine for reporting.

The focus of this chapter is on the "RunParser" engine; an understanding of the overall structure will help with the connecting relationships to the other engines.

The "RunGUI" Engine manages three rules: 1) File Manager, 2) the Lexer, and 3) the Parser. The File Manager opens the file and reads in the first record and if there are no issues jumps to the rLexr+5 step (see Table 10.0). The Lexer reads one character at a time from the File Manager and determines how it should respond to the character. From the Lexer's perspective there are five state conditions:

1) A control character. Those are the normal non-printing characters that range in decimal value from 0 to 31. This range includes tab, carriage return (newline), linefeed, and form feed.

2) The range of alpha characters from uppercase A-Z and lowercase a-z.

3) The characters that make up the numbers 0-9.

4) All of the other printing characters that make up the symbols and are treated as delimiters.

5) The last state condition is the end-of-line (EOL).

The "RunLexer" Engine determines the type of character then returns a value (token) that represents the character. This lexer recognizes four token types. If the character is a letter, then the token value becomes <iWord>. If the character is a space or comma then the token becomes <iDelimiter>. If the character is a number the token value becomes <iNumber>. The final type of token is the <iCtrl> that represents all of the non-printing control characters.

The "RunLexer" Engine continues processing characters, and creating words or numbers by concatenating the characters. Only when a defined delimiter is found does the "RunLexer" Engine stop scanning the record and send the token value to the "RunGUI" Engine. The "RunLexer" Engine doesn't return individual characters.

The trace file shows that while parsing a line, the "RunGUI" Engine loops from trace 111 to 116. When an end of record is reached, the application jumps from trae 116 to back to trace 111 and then finally back to trace 106, where it gets the next record. After this process is complete, the "RunGUI" Engine checks for issues between trace 107 and trace 110 and then processes the record as before from trace 111 to trace 116.

Rules	Static State	True Action	Next Rule	False Action	Next Rule	Trace
rFile,	iOpenFile	OpenText,	rFile+1,	Ignore,	rError,	100
rFile+1,	iGetLine,	GetLine,	rFile+2,	Ignore,	Error,	101
rFile+2,	iChkErr,	Read_Err,	rFile,	ChkRcLn,	rFile+3,	102
rFile+3,	iZeroRec,	ZeroRecd,	rLexr+5,	ChkEOF,	rFile+4,	103
rFile+4,	iEndOfF,	procDone,	rDone,	Ignore,	rFile+5,	104
rFile+5,	iAddNode,	AddNode,	rLexr+5,	procErr,	rError,	105
rLexr,	iGetLn,	GetLine,	rLexr+1,	Ignore,	rError,	106
rLexr+1,	iChkErr,	Read_Err,	rError,	ChkRcLn,	rLexr+2,	107
rLexr+2,	iZeroRec,	ZeroRecd,	rLexr,	ChkEOF,	rLexr+3,	108
rLexr+3,	iEndOfF,	procDone,	rDone,	Ignore,	rLexr+4,	109
rLexr+4,	iAddNode,	AddChild,	rLexr+5,	procErr,	rError,	110
rLexr+5,	iAnalyze	AnalyzeStr,	rPars,	Ignore,	rLexr,	111
rPars,	iWord,	CountWords,	rPars+2,	Ignore,	rPars+1,	112
rPars+1,	iTokNumb,	CountNumbs,	rPars+2,	Ignore,	rPars+2,	113
rPars+2,	iTokDelm,	Delimiters,	rPars+3,	Ignore,	rPars+4,	114
rPars+3,	iTokCtrl,	Control,	rPars+4,	Ignore,	rPars+5,	115
rPars+4,	iSetTokn,	SetToken,	rLexr+5,	Ignore,	rError,	116
rDone,	iDone,	procDone,	rDone,	procDone	rDone,	198
rError,	iError,	procErr,	rError,	procErr,	rError,	199

Table 10.0
RunGUI – Extended BNF Rules

The Phone Number Data File

The specification for the contents of the phone number data file includes people's names, phone numbers, the location or type of phone number, and occasionally a spouse's name. The names are listed as last name comma first name. The phone numbers are ten-digit numbers formatted with dashes and the option for each row to include extensions. The phone numbers are identified by location, including work, home, or cell. And the last column is the spouse's first name.

```
Bottomley,Mike,777-555-0123,x123,Home,Arija;
Gougler,Bill,303-555-0575,20,Work,Karen;
Kraieski,,770-555-8031,,Home,Nancy;
```
Sample from data file

Commas separate each of these fields. The phone number is one field with three values separated by dashes. Based an initial view of the file the "RunParser" Engine will see the following including the three optional fields.

Parser   = \<iWord> \<iDelimiter> \<iWord> \< iDelimiter >
\<iNumber> \< iDelimiter > \<iNumber> \< iDelimiter >
\<iNumber> \< iDelimiter > \<iNumber>? \< iDelimiter >
\<iWord>? \< iDelimiter > \<iWord>?;

The next step is to view the BNF in tree format and then to determine the actions of each of the returned tokens. The narrative is used to create the following logical layout.

Rule Step	Static State	True Action	False Action
Parser	<iWord>	LastName	Name1Err
	<iDelimiter>	Comma	SpaceError
	<iWord>	FirstName	Name2Err
	<iDelimiter>	Comma	DelimErr
	<iNumber>	AreaCode	AreaErr
	<iDelimiter>	Dash	DashErr
	<iNumber>	Prefix	PrefixErr
	<iDelimiter>	Dash	DashErr
	<iNumber>	Local	LocalErr
	<iDelimiter>	Comma	DelimErr
	<iNumber>	Exten?	ExtenErr
	<iDelimiter>	Comma	DelimErr
	<iWord>	Type?	TypeErr
	<iDelimiter>	Comma	DelimErr
	<iWord>	Spouse?	SpouseErr;

Table 10.1
Building the Parser Logic Tree

The token values for word <iWord> and number <iNumber> are sufficient for the current specification. The <iDelimiter> values need to be more specific since the actions are looking for comma and dash. In Table 10.2 where the true action is "Comma" the state is changed to <iComma>. Where the true action is "Dash" the state is changed to <iDash>.

The specification defines only three optional fields: extension, type, and spouse name. If these values do not exist, then their false action isn't an error. Those false actions are replaced with the Ignore behaviors to allow the parser to continue scanning the data record.

Rule Step	Static State	True Action	Next	False Action	Next	Trace
Parser	\<iWord>	LastName		Name1Err		
	\<iComma>	Comma		SpaceError		
	\<iWord>	FirstName		Name2Err		
	\< iComma>	Comma		DelimErr		
	\<iNumber>	AreaCode		AreaErr		
	\<iDash>	Dash		DashErr		
	\<iNumber>	Prefix		PrefixErr		
	\<iDash>	Dash		DashErr		
	\<iNumber>	Local		LocalErr		
	\< iComma>	Comma		DelimErr		
	\<iNumber>	Exten		**Ignore**		
	\< iComma>	Comma		DelimErr		
	\<iWord>	Type		**Ignore**		
	\< iComma>	Comma		DelimErr		
	\<iWord>	Spouse		**Ignore;**		

Table 10.2
Building the Parser Logic

If the dynamic token sent from the "RunLexer" Engine matches the expected static state in the "RunParser" Engine, then the transition is to the next state. If the token does not match what the "RunParser" Engine is expecting, then a simple solution is to transition to an appropriate error action, which could be just scanning to the end of the record.

If data is incorrect a more complex and controversial step is to try to clean up the data or set an agreed upon value into the record that indicates this is bad data. For example, suppose the first field contained a number. If this were the case, a subordinate engine could be instantiated to analyze the situation. Then an *asterisk* could be placed at the beginning of that field as an agreed upon indicator of bad data associated with the higher-level action "firstname".

When data is missing from the record there are limits on what can be done to recover the record. One possible approach would be to perform a syntactical analysis of the record and look for potential ways to fill in the record. Understanding the syntax of the record through the analysis of a subordinate engine could help reconstruct or pad the missing data to allow the scanner and parser to get back in sync.

The next step is to hook up the temporal component. It's a matter of defining the temporal rules, which looks like this. If a value does not exist in an optional field, like the optional phone extension number, the "Ignore" false action at "Parser+10" then the parser is only looking for the delimiters at "Parser+11".

Rule Step	Static State	True Action	Next True	False Action	Next False	Trace
Parser	<iWord>	LastName	Parser+1	Name1Err	Parser+1	
+1	<iComma>	Comma	Parser+2	SpaceError	Parser+2	
+2	<iWord>	FirstName	Parser+3	Name2Err	Parser+3	
+3	< iComma>	Comma	Parser+4	DelimErr	Parser+4	
+4	<iNumber>	AreaCode	Parser+5	AreaErr	Parser+5	
+5	<iDash>	Dash	Parser+6	DashErr	Parser+6	
+6	<iNumber>	Prefix	Parser+7	PrefixErr	Parser+7	
+7	<iDash>	Dash	Parser+8	DashErr	Parser+8	
+8	<iNumber>	Local	Parser+9	LocalErr	Parser+9	
+9	< iComma>	Comma	Parser+10	DelimErr	Parser+10	
+10	<iNumber>	Exten	Parser+11	**Ignore**	Parser+11	
+11	< iComma>	Comma	Parser+12	DelimErr	Parser+12	
+12	<iWord>	Type	Parser+13	**Ignore**	Parser+13	
+13	< iComma>	Comma	Parser+14	DelimErr	Parser+14	
+14	<iWord>	Spouse	Parser	**Ignore;**	Parser	

Table 10.3
Building the Parser Logic

A limited number of errors will be fixed if they show up and marked with an error character. At some predetermined count the file will be declared as corrupt and processing would stop. The "continue to process" actions can be determined by the incremental sequence of the "Next False" temporal step, which will continue down the rule progression using the false "*Err" actions to do the filling in and counting errors. The actual implementation of the rules is below.

Rules Step	Static State	True Action	Next Rule	False Action	Next Rule	Trace
rPars,	<iWord>	FirstName,	rPars+1,	Name1Err,	rPars+1,	3000
rPars+1,	<iComma>	WhiteSpace	rPars+2,	ParseErr,	rPars+2,	3001
rPars+2,	<iWord>	LastName,	rPars+3,	Name2Err,	rPars+3,	3002
rPars+3,	< iComma>	Comma,	rPars+4,	ParseErr,	rPars+4,	3003
rPars+4,	<iNumber>	Area,	rPars+5,	CodeErr,	rPars+5,	3004
rPars+5,	<iDash>	Dash,	rPars+6,	ParseErr,	rPars+6,	3005
rPars+6,	<iNumber>	Prefix,	rPars+7,	PrefErr,	rPars+7,	3006
rPars+7,	<iDash>	Dash,	rPars+8,	ParseErr,	rPars+8,	3007
rPars+8,	<iNumber>	Local,	rPars+9,	NumbErr,	rPars+9,	3008
rPars+9,	< iComma>	Comma,	rPars+10,	ParseErr,	rPars+10,	3009
rPars+10,	<iNumber>	Extn,	rPars+11,	Ignore,	rPars+11,	3008
rPars+11,	< iComma>	Comma,	rPars+12,	ParseErr,	rPars+12,	3009
rPars+12,	<iWord>	Location,	rPars+13,	Ignore,	rPars+13,	3010
rPars+13,	< iComma>	Comma,	rPars+14,	ParseErr,	rPars+14,	3011
rPars+14,	<iWord>	SpouseName,	rPars,	Ignore,	rPars,	3012

Table 10.4
Data Parser Extended BNF Rules

Throwing a Wrench in the Works

As the logic has been defined the data parser application works fine. In the first record the name was changed to "M9." In the next record the second name was removed, leaving two commas back-to-back. The data parser application was tested and it failed. It failed for two reasons. First, in the parser table there are no token definitions for combined letters and numbers. And second there is no recovery rule to handle a delimiter followed by a delimiter when the second name is missing. The error action reports the error and continues through the rule.

134

Solving the Dilemma

The "RunLexer" Engine sets a token value when it receives the first character. If the first character was a letter and the second character was a number then the "RunLexer" Engine changes the letter token to a number token after it receives the first number. This is regardless of where Lexer Engine is in the process of building a name. In my original design, I kept the internal building areas separate as I did in the calculator so I did not get an error trying to convert "M9" into a number. Logically it isn't known if a word will contain numbers or any other characters in a data stream until they are encountered.

As was mentioned in Chapter 1, this is the dilemma: Without using if-then-else, how is this problem solved?

To solve the problem, I added two new temporal rules to the GUI rules. The step at "rPars+2" is added to handle words that contain numbers. The rule at "rPars+5" was added to handle a null data field. I added two support routines to handle the new state of "word with numbers."

The first support routine combines the current token with the digit token. This routine is placed in each of the number Lexer routines 0 through 9. The token for a word is a "1". The token for a number is a "2". The token for a number-word is a "3". When logically OR'd "1" and "2", the result is the token for number-word "3". The second routine is "ClearToken." This routine is added to the Lexer Engine and is called from the "RunGUI" Engine by the "Empty" behavior, by the "Delimiters" behavior, and by the "Control" behavior. The dilemma is solved without the use of ITE.

Static Rules	True State	Next Action	False Rule	Next Action	Rule	Trace
rFile,	iOpenFile,	OpenText,	rFile+1,	Ignore,	rError,	100
rFile+1,	iGetLine,	GetLine,	rFile+2,	Ignore,	rError,	101
rFile+2,	iChkErr,	Read_Err,	rFile,	ChkRcLn,	rFile+3,	102
rFile+3,	iZeroRec,	ZeroRecd,	rLexr+5,	ChkEOF,	rFile+4,	103
rFile+4,	iEndOfF,	procDone,	rDone,	Ignore,	rFile+5,	104
rFile+5,	iAddNode,	AddNode,	rLexr+5,	procErr,	rError,	105
rLexr,	iGetLn,	GetLine,	rLexr+1,	Ignore,	rError,	106
rLexr+1,	iChkErr,	Read_Err,	rError,	ChkRcLn,	rLexr+2,	107
rLexr+2,	iZeroRec,	ZeroRecd,	rLexr,	ChkEOF,	rLexr+3,	108
rLexr+3,	iEndOfF,	procDone,	rDone,	Ignore,	rLexr+4,	109
rLexr+4,	iAddNode,	AddChild,	rLexr+5,	procErr,	rError,	110
rLexr+5,	iAnalyze,	AnalyzeStr,	rPars,	Ignore,	rLexr,	111
rPars,	iWord,	CountWords,	rPars+3,	Ignore,	rPars+1,	112
rPars+1,	iTokNumb,	CountNumbs,	rPars+3,	Ignore,	rPars+2,	113
rPars+2,	**iTokWdNm,**	**CountWords,**	**rPars+3,**	**Ignore,**	**rPars+3,**	**114**
rPars+3,	iTokDelm,	Delimiters,	rPars+6,	Ignore,	rPars+4,	115
rPars+4,	iTokCtrl,	**Control,**	rPars+6,	Ignore,	rPars+5,	116
rPars+5,	**iEmpty,**	**Empty,**	**rPars+6,**	**Ignore,**	**rError,**	**117**
rPars+6,	iSetTokn,	SetToken,	rLexr+5,	Ignore,	rError,	118
rDone,	iDone,	procDone,	rDone,	procDone	rDone,	198
rError,	iError,	procErr,	rError,	procErr,	rError,	199

Table 10.5
Data Parser Extended BNF Rules

The data parser is tested with the new logic against the data file that contains words with mixed letters and numbers and back-to-back delimiters. The application runs through to completion reporting what it found. In Figure 10.0 below the first record has an extension and the third record is missing the name after "Kraieski".

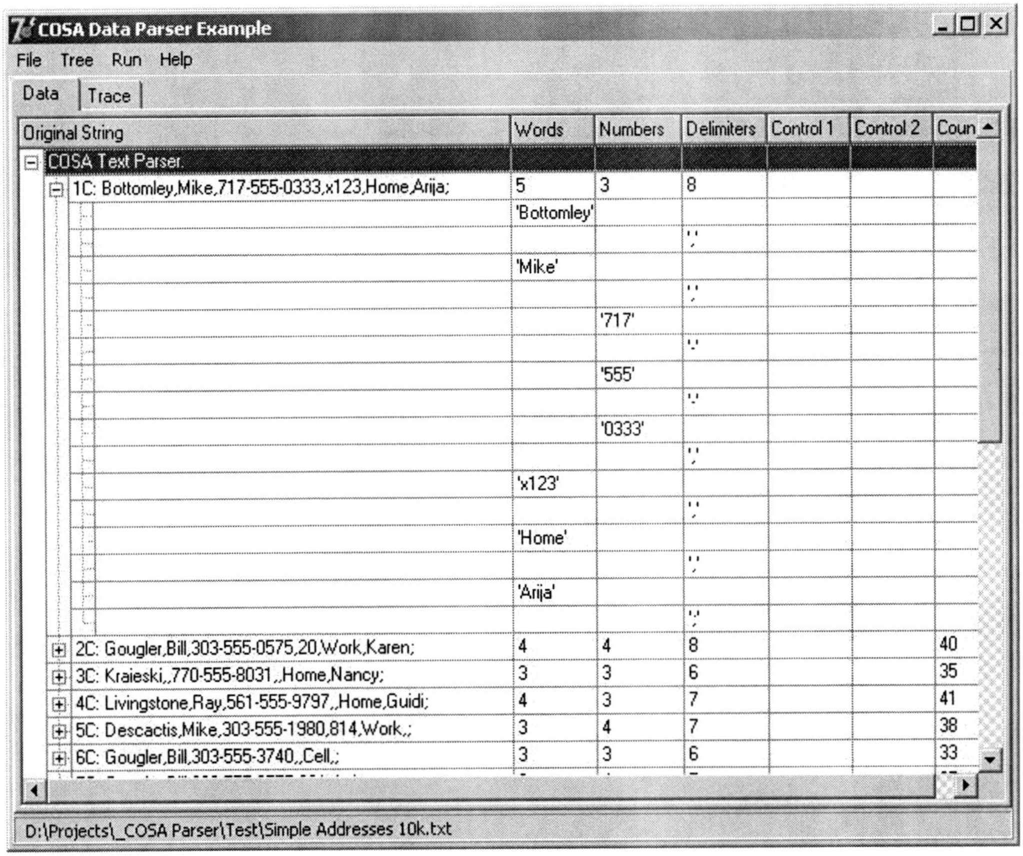

Figure 10.0
COSA Data Parser Application – Data Tree Display

The data parser listbox shows the original line of data. The other columns in the listbox count words, numbers, and delimiters and display them in a tree for the data steward to review. Because the logic is separate from the manipulation of the data it is easy to add counters and other functionality without the additional logic becoming a "patch" on a "patch" like with the ITE ad hoc calculator.

Summary

Rules associated with business logic are easier to understand when the temporal aspect is shown directly in the program logic. Furthermore, this example shows how logic can be used to replace more complex parts of an application without resorting to the ITE approach.

It is relatively easy to clean up data using the COSA approach. This example can be expanded to be a very strong data filter in data migration applications producing SQL records or XML to an Internet application.

138

11

Chapter 11 – The COSA Stopwatch Example

The stopwatch is a good example because others have used it to show how to create a state machine. It also provides a simple task that can be handled in a single chapter. And it helps to have an example from the one of the leading computer science schools: Carnegie Mellon University – Software Engineering Institute[46] (CMU-SEI). The CME-SEI example stopwatch uses *three* buttons. To make the logic more interesting this chapter will demonstrate two different implementations using four-button and two-button stopwatches.

The Four-Button Stopwatch

The first stopwatch has **four** buttons (Figure 11.0) each button will perform a single function.

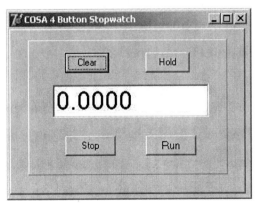

Figure 11.0
Four-Button Stopwatch

[46] "Personal Software Process for Engineers: Part II, Designing and Verifying State Machines", Sponsored by the US Department of Defense. PowerPoint Presentation, Pg 38 of "L7 State Machines.ppt".

The button names where chosen to correspond to the state. The Clear state is the initial state. *After the initial state* the following logic applies. The **clear** button clears the stopwatch at any time in its function from the Hold state, the Run state, or the Stop state.

Pressed Button	Current State	to	Next State
Run	Clear	to	Run
Run	Hold	to	Run
Stop	Hold	to	Stop
Clear	Hold	to	Clear
Hold	Run	to	Hold
Stop	Run	to	Stop
Clear	Run	to	Clear
Run	Stop	to	Run
Clear	Stop	to	Clear

The **hold** button allows the timer thread to continue running and keeps track of time while the stopwatch displays the time duration passed at the time the **hold** button was pushed. The only way to enter the Hold state is from the Run state. The Run state can be entered from the Clear state, the Hold state, or the Stop state by pressing the **run** button. The Stop state can only be entered from the Run state by pressing the **stop** button. There are nine possible valid transitions by this specification.

Borland Delphi version 7 was used to create the 4 Button Stopwatch Application to test the logic and produce the trace for discussions. Visio was used to create the CMU-SEI like stopwatch state chart in Figure 11.1 as a general reference for this problem. Valid logic transitions in the direction of the arrows from one state to the next.

140

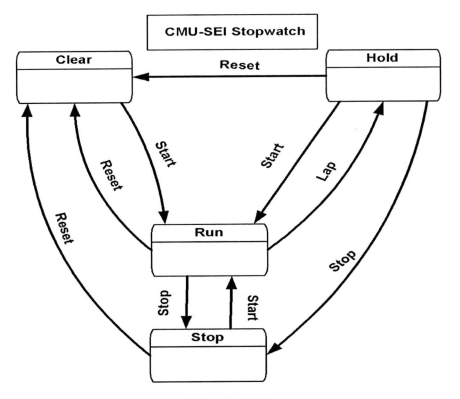

Figure 11.1
CMU-SEI Stopwatch Statechart

A comprehensive application needs to include rules to prevent any invalid request. From the state diagram[47] in Figure 11.1 it can be determined that there would be three such possible invalid transition requests represented by the *absence* of arrows. These invalid transitions are:

	Start State	to	Button Pushed
1)	Clear	to	Stop
2)	Clear	to	Hold
3)	Stop	to	Hold

---

[47] "Personal Software Process for Engineers: Part II, Designing and Verifying State Machines", Sponsored by the US Department of Defense. PowerPoint Presentation, Pg 38 of "L7 State Machines.ppt".

If the stopwatch is in the Clear state and the **stop** button is pressed the stopwatch should not respond and should remain in the Clear state. In this implementation as a digital stopwatch it can display an error message when an invalid state is entered.

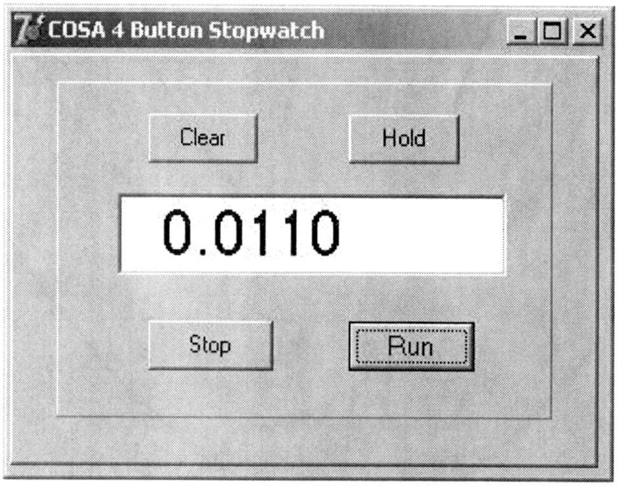

Figure 11.2
Four-Button Stopwatch

The rules that prevent invalid actions can be thought of as gatekeeper rules allowing or preventing a new state transition from occurring. When the event is prevented the gatekeeper returns the request to the previous valid state. The stopwatch always starts in the Clear state and transitions through its gatekeepers from there.

Using the CMU-SEI statechart Figure 11.1 the following BNF is produced for the COSA four-button stopwatch.

Stopwatch   = <rClear> | <rHold> | <rRun> | <rStop>;

The Clear state can only transition to one other state.

rClear   = <rRun>;

The Hold state can transition to three other states.

rHold   = <rRun> | <rStop> | <rClear> ;

The Run state can transition to three other states.

rRun   = <rHold> | <rStop> | <rClear>;

And finally, the Stop state can transition to the Run state or the Hold state.

rStop   = <rRun> | <rClear>;

The completed four rules and steps in BNF for the stopwatch are as follows:

Stopwatch	= <rClear>	<rHold>	<rRun>	<rStop>;
rClear (100)	= <rRun>;
rHold (200)	= <rRun>	<rStop>	<rClear> ;
rRun (300)	= <rHold>	<rStop>	<rClear>;
rStop (400)	= <rRun>	< rClear>;

Tree 11.0
Stopwatch – Extended BNF

The complete COSA Extended BNF Rules Table 11.0 has nine steps to create the stopwatch functionality using four buttons. These nine steps correspond directly to the nine possible transitions. The false logic (that is when the dynamic state does not match the static state) is used to transition in the search for a valid next state or to handle the error message for an invalid request. The rule "rClear" is only looking for the <iRun> state and reports an error if any other button is pushed.

Start Rule	Static State	True Action	Next True	False Action	Next False	Trace
rClear	<iRun>	pStart	rRun	pError	rClear	100
rHold	<iRun>	pStart	rRun	pIgnore	rHold+1	200
+1	<iStop>	pStop	rStop	pIgnore	rHold+2	201
+2	<iClear>	pClear	rClear	pError	rHold	202
rRun	<iHold>	pHold	rHold	pIgnore	rRun+1	300
+1	<iStop>	pStop	rStop	pIgnore	rRun+2	301
+2	<iClear>	pClear	rClear	pError	rRun	302
rStop	<iRun>	pStart	rRun	pIgnore	rStop+1	400
+1	<iClear>	pClear	rStop	pError	rStop	401

Table 11.0
Four-Button Stopwatch Rules – COSA Extended BNF

Backwards "Come From" Logic

The state chart in Figure 11.3 represents a backward "come from" logic. The valid initial states that can be considered in order to transition to the next state are listed on the right. The target valid states are on the left. The solid arrow is a true/valid transition from one of the listed states. There are nine solid arrows in this diagram representing all transitions that are valid. The dashed arrow represents the path taken for an invalid request searching for a valid transition.

144

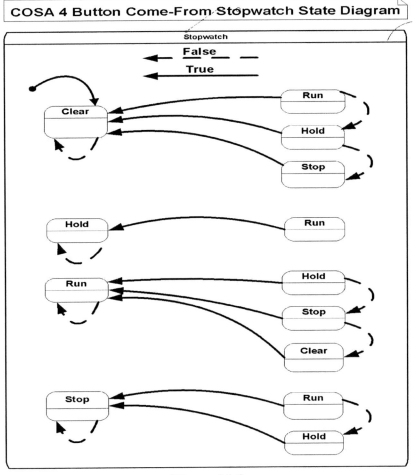

Figure 11.3
Backwards "Come-From" State Chart

The Clear state can be entered coming from the Run state. The Clear state can be entered coming from the Hold state. And finally, the Clear state can be entered coming from the Stop state. The Clear state returns to itself if an invalid Clear button is pressed, displaying an error message.

Forward "Go To" Logic

The forward logic seen in figure 11.4 is less complex and looks exactly like the COSA Extended BNF Rules Table. The state diagram is just a different view. The box on the left represents the rule name or the state that the stopwatch is in. The Clear state is only allowed to transition to the Run state; any other attempt will cause the digital stopwatch to display an error. There are nine solid arrows in this diagram representing valid transitions.

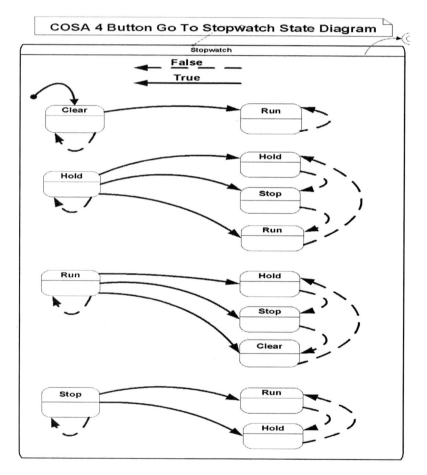

Figure 11.4
Foreword "Go To" State Chart

The CMU-SEI Corrected State Template

The "corrected" three-button stopwatch example[48] used by SEI shows eleven transition states in Table 11.1. When SEI produced the Corrected State Template shown below there were still two errors. The first error is at step 1: the State "Clear" and the Next State "- Clear". This is the initial state condition. Pressing the **clear** button would result in an ignore logic based on the state diagram provided with the problem. Yet SEI has made this a state transition in their logic table. In order for this transition to be correct the state diagram would need a loop-back condition, which is not provided.

Step	State	Next State	Transition Condition	Action
1)	Clear	- Clear	Reset v Hold	Stop / reset clock / clear display
2)		- Running	Start/Stop	Start / display clock
3)	Running	- Clear	Reset	Stop / reset clock / clear display
4)		- Hold	Hold	Hold display
5)		- Stopped	Start/Stop	Stop clock / hold display
6)	On-Hold	- Clear	Reset	Stop / reset clock / clear display
7)		- Running	Hold	Start /display clock
8)		- Stopped	Start/Stop	Stop clock / hold display
9)	Stopped	- Clear	Reset	Stop / reset clock / clear display
10)		- Running	Start/Stop	Start clock / display clock
11)		- Stopped	Hold	Stop clock / hold display

Table 11.1
SEI Corrected State Template – Three Button Transitions

The second mistake is a similar piece of logic. At Step 11 the State "Stopped" followed by the Transition Condition "Hold". Again the state chart does not have a transition arrow from the "Stopped" state to the "- Stopped" state. In addition the

---

[48] "Personal Software Process for Engineers: Part II, Designing and Verifying State Machines", Sponsored by the US Department of Defense. PowerPoint Presentation, Pg 52 of "L7 State Machines.ppt".

PowerPoint presentation provided by SEI[49] specifically points out that it is an invalid transition. This is a case in point about how important it is to stay synchronized using the base BNF to provide consistent information throughout the analysis and design.

The Two-Button Stopwatch

A digital wristwatch uses two buttons for its stopwatch function once the stopwatch mode has been selected. One button provides the **start/stop** control and the other button proves the **hold/clear** function. Initially the dynamic state on the wristwatch stopwatch is set to the Stop state. The only button that can be clicked for a response is the **start/stop** button. Clicking on the **hold/clear** button would fail to get a response.

When the stopwatch is running pressing the **run/stop** button again will result in the stopwatch being stopped. If the stopwatch is running and the **hold/clear** button is pushed, then the Hold rule would be executed and the stopwatch would transition to the Hold state. Pushing the **hold/clear** button a second time results in the stopwatch transitioning to the Clear state, clearing the display.

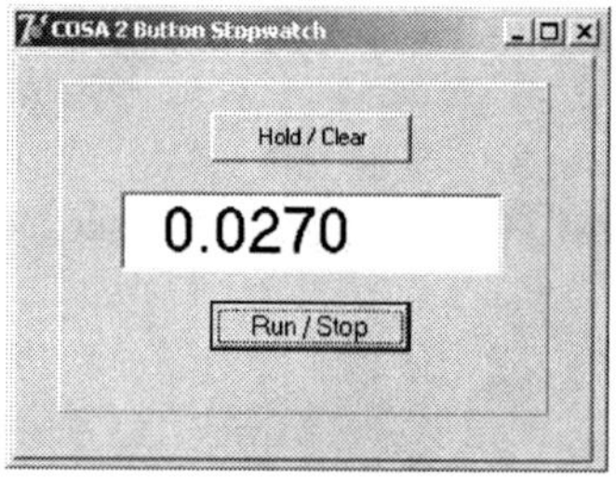

Figure 11.5
Two-Button Stopwatch

Summarized below are the five current states that the two-button stopwatch can be in. When one of the buttons is pushed the stopwatch will transition to its next state.

[49] "Personal Software Process for Engineers: Part II, Designing and Verifying State Machines", Sponsored by the US Department of Defense. PowerPoint Presentation, Pg 52 of "L7 State Machines.ppt".

	Current State		Button Pushed	
1)	Stop	to	Run	
2)	Run	to	Hold	}
3)	Run	to	Stop	} these two are consolidated into rule rRun
4)	Hold	to	Clear	
5)	Clear	to	Run	

Table 11.2
Two Button Transitions

The logic in the COSA Extended BNF Rules Table 11.3 describes these four states and their five transitions listed above.

Start Rule	Static State	True Action	Next	False Action	Next	Trace
rStop,	<iRun>	StpDisplay,	rRun,	Ignore,	rRun,	100
rRun,	<iRun>	RunDisplay,	rStop,	Ignore,	rHold,	200
rHold,	<iHold>	HldDisplay,	rClear,	Ignore,	rClear,	300
rClear,	<iHold>	ClrDisplay,	rHold,	Ignore,	rRun,	400

Table 11.3
Two-Button Stopwatch – COSA Extended BNF

It is interesting to note the differences between the four-button stopwatch rules and the two-button stopwatch rules. The logic of all of the nine rules of the four-button stopwatch is accomplished using only four lines of logic for the two-button stopwatch. In order for this logic to work the logic must transition through the "invalid" transitions shown in bold in Table 11.4 on lines 2, 3, and 9. For example, when the two-button stopwatch is in the <iHold> state and the **run** button is pressed. Then the logic must transition from <iHold> as false to "rClear" as false then to "rRun" as true.

Step	Four-Button	Two-Button	Four-Button Function
1)	Clear to Run	Clear to Run	
2)	Hold to Run		**Hold-Clear to Run**
3)	Hold to Stop		**Hold-Clear to Run-Stop**
4)	Hold to Clear	Hold to Clear	
5)	Run to Hold	Run to Hold	
6)	Run to Stop	Run to Stop	
7)	Run to Clear	Run to Clear	
8)	Stop to Run	Stop to Run	
9)	Stop to Clear		**Stop-Hold to Clear**

Table 11.4
Comparison of Four vs. Two Button Transitions

When the stopwatch is in the Hold state and the user presses the **run/stop** button the two-button stopwatch will transition from the Hold state through the Clear state to the Run state. This is equivalent to the Hold to Run state transition of the four-button stopwatch.

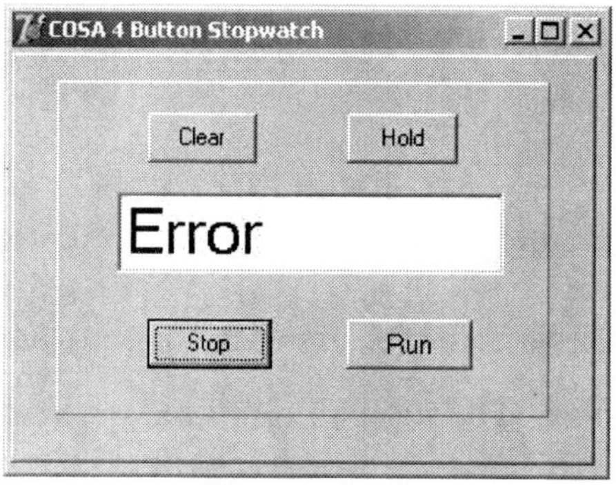

Figure 11.6
Four-Button Stopwatch

There are four conditions in Table 11.5 that will report an error with the four-button stopwatch Figure 11.6. One: the "rClear" rule and pressing any button but **run**. Two: the "rHold" rule and pressing the **hold** button. Three: the "rRun" rule and pressing the **run** button. Four: the "rStop" rule and pressing the **stop** or **hold** buttons.

150

	Rule	Static State	True	Next	False	Next	Trace
Start→	rClear	<iRun>	Start	rRun	Error	rClear	100
	rHold	<iRun>	Start	rRun	Ignore	rHold+1	200
	+1	<iStop>	Stop	rStop	Ignore	rHold+2	201
	+2	<iClear>	Clear	rClear	Error	rHold	202
	rRun	<iHold>	Hold	rHold	Ignore	rRun+1	300
	+1	<iStop>	Stop	rStop	Ignore	rRun+2	301
	+2	<iClear>	Clear	rClear	Error	rRun	302
	rStop	<iRun>	Start	rRun	Ignore	rStop+1	400
	+1	<iClear>	Clear	rStop	Error	rStop	401

Table 11.5
Four-Button Stopwatch Rules – COSA Extended BNF

The Four-Button Stopwatch Trace Analysis

The Trace File 11.0 provides a view of the logic in action. The first-column in the trace file indicates a true or false match between the third and fourth columns. The third-column is the dynamic state created by pressing a button on the stopwatch. The dynamic state is compared to the fourth-column, which is the static state that comes from the COSA Extended BNF Rules Table. The fifth-column is the trace number corresponding to the trace column in the COSA Rules Table. The sixth-column is the actual name of the true behavior as implemented. And the seventh-column is the name of the button pressed.

The "< >" between the Dynamic and Static columns indicates when a request was made by pressing a button for which the Dynamic does not match the Static. The subsequent logic then does a search to find a match and, if not found, reports an error Figure 11.6 on the digital stopwatch display.

T/F	Time	Dynamic		Static	Trace	T-Behavior	Button
T	00;	33;		33;	100;	RunDisplay	Run
T	04;	22;		22;	300;	HldDisplay	Hold
T	01;	33;		33;	200;	RunDisplay	Run
F	04;	44;	< >	22;	300		Stop
T	05;	44;		44;	301;	StpDisplay	
T	07;	33;		33;	400;	RunDisplay	Run
T	04;	22;		22;	300;	HldDisplay	Hold
F	01;	11;	< >	33;	200		Clear
F	02;	11;	< >	44;	201		
T	03;	11;		11;	202;	ClrDisplay	
T	00;	33;		33;	100;	RunDisplay	Run
F	04;	11;	< >	22;	300		
F	05;	11;	< >	44;	301		
T	06;	11;		11;	302;	ClrDisplay	Clear
F	00;	44;	< >	33;	100		
F	00;	11;	< >	33;	100		
F	00;	22;	< >	33;	100		
T	00;	33;		33;	100;	RunDisplay	Run
F	04;	11;	< >	22;	300		
F	05;	11;	< >	44;	301		
T	06;	11;		11;	302;	ClrDisplay	Clear
F	00;	22;	< >	33;	100		
T	00;	33;		33;	100;	RunDisplay	Run
F	04;	11;	< >	22;	300		
F	05;	11;	< >	44;	301		
T	06;	11;		11;	302;	ClrDisplay	Clear
F	00;	44;	< >	33;	100;		

Trace File 11.0
COSA Four-Button Runtime Trace

The first step in the trace shows the stopwatch running: Dynamic equals Static. The second step shows the stopwatch in the <iHold> state 22. The third state transitions back to the <iRun> state 33. In the fourth step the **stop** button is pressed and the stopwatch transitions through the <iHold> state 22, to the <iStop> state 44. From the stop state the **run** button is pressed and the stopwatch transitions to the <iRun> state 33. The **hold** button is then pressed followed by the **clear** button, these two buttons cause the states to transition from <iRun>, to <iStop>, to <iClear>.

The Two-Button Stopwatch Trace Analysis

The trace file format is the same for the two-button stopwatch. The trace numbers are different since each state has only one associated rule.

	Rule	Static State	True Action	Next	False Action	Next	Trace
Start→	rClear,	\<iHold\>	ClrDisplay,	rHold,	Ignore,	rRun,	100
	rHold,	\<iHold\>	HldDisplay,	rClear,	Ignore,	rClear,	200
	rRun,	\<iRun\>	RunDisplay,	rStop,	Ignore,	rHold,	300
	rStop,	\<iRun\>	StpDisplay,	rRun,	Ignore,	rRun,	400

Table 11.3
Two-Button Stopwatch –COSA Extended BNF

The initial state is set to \<iHold\>. When a button is pressed the dynamic state becomes either \<iRun\> or \<iHold\>. From Table 11.3 pressing the **run/stop** button caused the stopwatch to transition from the "rClear" to the "rRun" rule. Pressing the **run/stop** button for the second time will cause the stopwatch to transition from the "rRun" rule to the "rStop" rule, which executes the true action and stops the display. Pressing the **run/stop** button a third time will cause the stopwatch to transition to the "rRun" rule again. Pressing the **hold/clear** button will cause the stopwatch to transition to the "rHold" rule. Pressing the **run/stop** button will cause the stopwatch to transition to the "rClear" rule as false then back to the "rRun" rule. Where the stopwatch will continue running.

One strong disadvantage to the two-button stopwatch is the possibility of accidentally hitting the **hold/clear** button twice clearing a timed event or accidentally hitting the **run/stop** button twice not getting the correct time on an event. But from the perspective of the logic the two-button stopwatch is very simple.

Trace File 11.1 provides the trace coverage of several operations of the various functions in the two-button stopwatch. The "<>" between the Dynamic and Static column indicates where there was not a match in the logic request.

Clear = 11; Hold = 22; Run = 33; Stop = 44;

T/F	Time	Dynamic		Static	Trace	Button
T	01;	33;		33;	300;	Run
T	00;	33;		33;	400;	Stop
T	01;	33;		33;	300;	Run
T	00;	33;		33;	400;	Stop
T	01;	33;		33;	300;	Run
T	00;	33;		33;	400;	Stop
F	01;	22;	<>	33;	300	
T	02;	22;		22;	200;	Hold
F	03;	33;	<>	22;	100	
T	01;	33;		33;	300;	Run
T	00;	33;		33;	400;	Stop
F	01;	22;	<>	33;	300	
T	02;	22;		22;	200;	Hold
F	03;	33;	<>	22;	100	
T	01;	33;		33;	300;	Run
T	00;	33;		33;	400;	Stop
T	01;	33;		33;	300;	Run
F	00;	22;	<>	33;	400	
F	01;	22;	<>	33;	300	
T	02;	22;		22;	200;	Hold
T	03;	22;		22;	100;	Clear

Trace File 11.1
COSA Two-Button Runtime Trace

Two-Button Stopwatch Delphi Implementation

The Delphi library information and class definitions are in the preamble section of the application.

```delphi
unit StopWatch2Unit;

interface

uses
  Windows, Messages, SysUtils, Variants, Classes, Graphics, Controls,
  Forms, Dialogs, StdCtrls, ExtCtrls, ComCtrls;

type
// ********************** COSA Rule Structure **********************
  pProcedureType = procedure of Object;
  fButtonType = function : TObject;
  TCOSARules = class
  public
  private
          iTime : integer;
          iState : integer;
          pTrueRule : pProcedureType;
          iTrueRule : integer;
          pFalseRule : pProcedureType;
          iFalseRule : integer;
          iTrace : integer;
  end;

//********************* COSA Framework for Rules to Run In **********

  TstopwatchForm = class(TForm)
    PageControl1: TPageControl;
    Panel1: TPanel;
    listboxStopWatch: TListBox;
    buttonRunStop: TButton;
    buttonHoldClr: TButton;
    procedure buttonHoldClr_OnClick(Sender: TObject);
    procedure buttonRunStop_OnClick(Sender: TObject);
    procedure StopWatchForm_OnCreate(Sender: TObject);
    procedure formCloseFile_OnClose(Sender: TObject;
      var Action: TCloseAction);
  private
    { Private declarations }
  public
    { Public declarations }
    procedure Run(intState: integer);
```

```
private
  dynamicState, iTime, iStart : integer;
  iClear, iHold, iRun, iStop : integer;
  rClear, rHold, rRun, rStop : integer;
  bEngine : boolean;
  fNumber, fDisplay : real;
  pOperArg00 : pProcedureType;
  sNumber : String;
  TRACE_FILE : TextFile;
  strAction : Array [0..3] of String;   // for the Action names
  rRule : Array [0..3] of TCOSARules;    // the logic

  procedure pMCM(iTime : integer; iState : integer;
          pTrueRule : pProcedureType; iTrueRule : integer;
          pFalseRule : pProcedureType; iFalseRule : integer;
          iTrace : integer);     // used for dynamic initialization
  procedure True_Trace(iTime : integer);
  procedure False_Trace(iTime : integer);
  procedure CreateRules();
  procedure Error();
  procedure Ignore();
  procedure ClrDisplay();
  procedure HldDisplay();
  procedure RunDisplay();
  procedure StpDisplay();
end;
var
  stopwatchForm : TstopwatchForm;
```

The Stopwatch COSA Engine

The Delphi application logic section for the runtime engine, the procedures, and the logic table.

```
implementation
{$R *.dfm}

procedure TstopwatchForm.Run(intState: integer);
begin
  bEngine := TRUE;
  dynamicState := intState;
  while bEngine do                        // Preemption control
  begin
    if dynamicState = rRule[iTime].iState then// State Logic Control
      begin
        rRule[iTime].pTrueRule;           // True Cohesive Behavior
        True_Trace(iTime);                // True Trace and Debug
        iTime := rRule[iTime].iTrueRule;  // True Next Time Logic
      end else
      begin
        rRule[iTime].pFalseRule;          // False Cohesive Behavior
        False_Trace(iTime);               // False Trace and Debug
        iTime := rRule[iTime].iFalseRule; // False Next Time Logic
      end;
  end;
end;

procedure TstopwatchForm.CreateRules();
begin
```

//			Next		False		
//		Static	True	True	False	Next	
//	Rules	State	Behavior	Rule	Behavior	Rule	Trace
pMCM(rClear,	iHold,	ClrDisplay,	rHold,	Ignore,	rRun,	100);	
pMCM(rHold,	iHold,	HldDisplay,	rClear,	Ignore,	rClear,	200);	
pMCM(rRun,	iRun,	RunDisplay,	rStop,	Ignore,	rHold,	300);	
pMCM(rStop,	iRun,	StpDisplay,	rRun,	Ignore,	rRun,	400);	

```
end;
```

```
procedure TstopwatchForm.ClrDisplay();
begin
    sNumber := '0';
    fNumber := 0.0;
    StopTimer();
    listboxStopWatch.Items.Clear;
    listboxStopWatch.Items.Add('0.0000');
    bEngine := FALSE;
end;

procedure TstopwatchForm.HldDisplay();
begin
    fNumber := GetTimer();
    listboxStopWatch.Items.Clear;
    sNumber := Format('%8.4f', [fNumber]);
    listboxStopWatch.Items.Add(sNumber);
    bEngine := FALSE;
end;

procedure TstopwatchForm.RunDisplay();
begin
    fNumber := StartTimer();
    sNumber := Format('%8.4f', [fNumber]);
    listboxStopWatch.Items.Clear;
    listboxStopWatch.Items.Add(sNumber);
    bEngine := FALSE;
end;

procedure TstopwatchForm.StpDisplay();
begin
    fNumber := GetTimer();
    StopTimer();
    sNumber := Format('%8.4f', [fNumber]);
    listboxStopWatch.Items.Clear;
    listboxStopWatch.Items.Add(sNumber);
    bEngine := FALSE;
end;

procedure TstopwatchForm.Error();
begin
    listboxStopWatch.Items.Clear;
    listboxStopWatch.Items.Add('Error');
    bEngine := FALSE;
end;
```

```
procedure TstopwatchForm.pMCM(iTime : integer; iState : integer;
             pTrueRule : pProcedureType; iTrueRule : integer;
             pFalseRule : pProcedureType; iFalseRule : integer;
             iTrace : integer);
begin
  rRule[iTime] := TCOSARules.Create;
  rRule[iTime].iTime := iTime;
  rRule[iTime].iState := iState;
  rRule[iTime].pTrueRule := pTrueRule;
  rRule[iTime].iTrueRule := iTrueRule;
  rRule[iTime].pFalseRule := pFalseRule;
  rRule[iTime].iFalseRule := iFalseRule;
  rRule[iTime].iTrace := iTrace;
end;


procedure TstopwatchForm.True_Trace(iTime : integer);
var
  sTraceString : string;
begin
  sTraceString :=
          Format('T      %2.2d', [iTime]) +
          Format(';      %2.2d', [dynamicState]) +
          Format(';          %2.2d', [rRule[iTime].iState]) +
          Format(';      %3.3d;    ', [rRule[iTime].iTrace]) +
          strAction[iTime];
  Writeln(TRACE_FILE, sTraceString);
end;


procedure TstopwatchForm.False_Trace(iTime : integer);
var
  sTraceString : string;
begin
  sTraceString :=
          Format('F      %2.2d', [iTime]) +
          Format(';      %2.2d', [dynamicState]) +
          Format(';           %2.2d', [rRule[iTime].iState]) +
          Format(';      %3.3d', [rRule[iTime].iTrace]);
  Writeln(TRACE_FILE, sTraceString);
end;


procedure TstopwatchForm.Ignore();
begin
end;
```

```
procedure TstopwatchForm.buttonHoldClr_OnClick(Sender: TObject);
begin
    Run(iHold);            // Hold-Clear button on click event
end;


procedure TstopwatchForm.buttonRunStop_OnClick(Sender: TObject);
begin
    Run(iRun);             // Run-Stop on click event
end;


procedure TstopwatchForm.StopWatchForm_OnCreate(Sender: TObject);
begin
    AssignFile(TRACE_FILE, '_Stopwatch_2B_Trace.txt');
    Rewrite(TRACE_FILE);
    WriteLn(TRACE_FILE, 'Date= ' + DateToStr(Date));
    WriteLn(TRACE_FILE, 'Start of COSA 2 Button Stopwatch Trace
File.');
    WriteLn(TRACE_FILE, 'T/F,  Time,   Dynamic,   Static,   Trace');
    WriteLn(TRACE_FILE);
       rStop := 0; rRun := 1; rHold := 2; rClear := 3;
    sNumber := '0.0000';
       iClear := 11; iHold :=22; iRun := 33; iStop := 44;
    iTime := 1;
    strAction[0] := 'Stop';
    strAction[1] := 'Run';
    strAction[2] := 'Hold';
    strAction[3] := 'Clear';
    CreateRules();
end;


procedure TstopwatchForm.formCloseFile_OnClose(Sender: TObject;
  var Action: TCloseAction);
begin
    WriteLn(TRACE_FILE);
    WriteLn(TRACE_FILE, 'Close 2 Button Stopwatch Trace.');
    CloseFile(TRACE_FILE);
end;
end.
```

Summary

A CMU-SEI statechart and template provides the basic logic of a three-button stopwatch. The COSA BNF approach analyzes this information to produce a two-button and a four-button COSA stopwatch implementation.

The two-button stopwatch may be nearly the same as the four-button stopwatch functionally but does not provide nearly the coverage for reporting or handling potential errors. The reason is simple. The four steps in the two-button stopwatch can only focus on state transitions, not on checking errors. The four-button stopwatch has nine steps with four steps checking for errors resulting in a more robust coverage.

12

Chapter 12 – Moving Toward Better Software

There is a better way to produce software, but it takes getting past a lot of cultural barriers, the not invented here, the risk adverseness, and the tendency to take only evolutionary steps. To the senior engineer and managers here are six things I recommend:

1) Use BNF to define everything.   Everything you do will eventually become a well-defined BNF.

2) Expect time to be defined everywhere; even asynchronous events have a well-defined temporal component.

3) Follow the COSA paradigm for temporal engineering; spatial programming doesn't work, recognize it, and avoid it.

4) Don't succumb to the dark side of ITE, it leads to spatial programming. You can find the temporal logic using COSA that will make it work.

5) Demand the support you need to stay synchronized from the specification to testing; everyone wins with better quality reusable software.

6) It takes an engineering discipline. Avoid the shortcuts. Understand the logic. Just say no to ITE.

There are significant benefits to moving from an ad hoc approach to creating software to a very structured paradigm like COSA. With the COSA paradigm an industry will develop providing tools that will analyze the logic and the data manipulation in great detail. These tools will include multi-threaded analysis because COSA uses an orthogonal architecture. This analysis will have a much better understanding of the parallel threaded logic.

The Fundamentals

When the fundamentals of software development are as ad hoc as they currently are the industry has a problem. When software engineering is about the management of document control there aren't any fundamentals. With those two sentences I have probably stepped on a lot of toes, but I believe there have been many valid attempts to produce better software through standards, reuse, patterns, object tools, data tools, and many other things. As multi-core technology becomes the dominant processor technology and multi-threading becomes the way of getting more throughput, the core software development technology becomes even more important. The problem is that there aren't any core development technologies or paradigms. The good news is that COSA provides a core paradigm that can create significantly better quality software. Provided that the tenants of the COSA paradigm are not violated, the quality of companies using this new paradigm will begin to improve.

Epilogue

A well-formed communication is simple and elegant. The description of that communication can be diagrammed in BNF. The rules that make up business, engineering, science, government, law, or military tactics can be collected in a multitude of simple BNF definitions. These definitions become like the secret formula for Coke® well understood and guarded.

A significant amount of ambiguity can be removed from logic using a COSA Extended BNF approach. The task of moving billions of lines of spaghetti code into a COSA framework is not as daunting as it might seem, but it will never happen without a commitment to change at all levels.

The greatest challenge to better software is that people are very resistant to change[50]. People need to see a very gradual evolution in technology. Because this need for a gradual change is true, individuals and groups become a part of the "reluctance to change[51]" syndrome. History is full of stories about reluctance to change: the revolutionary concepts of germs, the sun at the center of the solar system, the copy machine, the automobile, computers, and many more. But once the change starts it will grow like wildfire.

As a taxpayer I would certainly like to see the software used by the government improved. Imagine what NSA, DARPA, NASA, NOAA, and the IRS could do with this technological improvement. The clandestine agencies

---

[50] Ernst von Glaserfeld, "The Reluctance to Change a Way of Thinking*", Irish Journal of Psychology, 1988.
[51] Linda Tucci, "Fear factor puts big chill on IT projects", 09 June 2005, SearchCIO.com, http://www.strysik.com/Lead_315_Reluctance_to_Change.html

should be open to investigate any improvements in software. All of these institutions should embrace change, especially if there is a significant chance an improvement will result.

Jiri Soukup the author of "The Inevitable Cycle: Graphical Tools and Programming Paradigms", *IEEE Computer*, August 2007, wrote; "Each time the idea of designing software with graphical tools becomes popular, a transition to a new, more powerful programming paradigm makes these tools obsolete. If this observation is correct, the Unified Modeling Language's current popularity indicates we're approaching the next major paradigm shift." Time will tell.

Lesson Learned

I've included on the next page the poem "The Calf Path" by Sam Walter Foss because I believe this is a good metaphor of how ITE software got started and why it still exists today. This poem certainly addresses the "reluctance to change."

The Calf Path

Sam Walter Foss (1858-1911)

One day through the primeval wood
A calf walked home as good calves should;
But made a trail all bent askew,
A crooked trail as all calves do.
Since then three hundred years have fled,
And I infer the calf is dead.

But still he left behind his trail,
And thereby hangs my moral tale.
The trail was taken up next day
By a lone dog that passed that way;
And then a wise bell-wether sheep
Pursued the trail o'er vale and steep,
And drew the flock behind him, too,
As good bell-wethers always do.

And from that day, o'er hill and glade,
Through those old woods a path was made,
And many men wound in and out,
And dodged and turned and bent about,
And uttered words of righteous wrath
Because 'twas such a crooked path;

But still they followed-do not laugh-
The first migrations of that calf,
And through this winding wood-way stalked
Because he wobbled when he walked.

This forest path became a lane,
That bent, and turned, and turned again.
This crooked lane became a road,
Where many a poor horse with his load
Toiled on beneath the burning sun,
And traveled some three miles in one.

And thus a century and a half
They trod the footsteps of that calf.
The years passed on in swiftness fleet.

The road became a village street;
And this, before men were aware,
A city's crowded thoroughfare,
And soon the central street was this
Of a renowned metropolis;
And men two centuries and a half
Trod in the footsteps of that calf.

Each day a hundred thousand rout
Followed this zigzag calf about,
And o'er his crooked journey went
The traffic of a continent.
A hundred thousand men were led
By one calf near three centuries dead.

They followed still his crooked way,
And lost one hundred years a day,
For thus such reverence is lent
To well-established precedent.
A moral lesson this might teach
Were I ordained and called to preach;

For men are prone to go it blind
Along the calf-paths of the mind,
And work away from sun to sun
To do what other men have done.
They follow in the beaten track,
And out and in, and forth and back,
And still their devious course pursue,
To keep the path that others do.

They keep the path a sacred groove,
Along which all their lives they move;
But how the wise old wood-gods laugh,
Who saw the first primeval calf.
Ah, many things this tale might teach-
But I am not ordained to preach.

Appendix A – COSA Trace File

Static and Dynamic States: Add = 44; Sub = 43; Mul = 42; Div = 47;

Digit = 1; Negate = 44; Period = 59;

Count	Step	Trace	Eng	Static	Dynamic	Behavior	Value
1	+T= 0;	100	Off;	44;	44;	Negate;	N= -
2	+T= 1;	101	Off;	1;	1;	Any_Number;	N= -3
3	−F= 1;	101	On;	1;	59;	Ignore;	N=
4	+T= 2;	102	Off;	59;	59;	One_Period;	N= -3.
5	+T= 3;	103	Off;	1;	1;	Any_Number;	N= -3.1
6	+T= 3;	103	Off;	1;	1;	Any_Number;	N= -3.14
7	+T= 3;	103	Off;	1;	1;	Any_Number;	N= -3.141
8	+T= 3;	103	Off;	1;	1;	Any_Number;	N= -3.1415
9	+T= 3;	103	Off;	1;	1;	Any_Number;	N= -3.14159
10	−F= 3;	103	On;	1;	44;	Ignore;	N=
11	−F= 4;	104	On;	12;	44;	Ignore;	N=
12	−F= 5;	105	On;	11;	44;	Ignore;	N=
13	−F= 6;	106	On;	1;	44;	Push_Disp;	N=
14	−F= 7;	500	On;	43;	44;	Ignore;	N=
15	+T= 8;	501	On;	44;	1;	Subtraction;	N= -3.14159
16	+T= 12;	700	Off;	1;	1;	Engine_Off;	N= -3.14159
17	+T= 13;	701	Off;	44;	44;	Negate;	N= -
18	+T= 14;	702	Off;	1;	1;	Any_Number;	N= -2
19	−F= 14;	702	Off;	1;	59;	Ignore;	N=
20	+T= 15;	703	Off;	59;	59;	One_Period;	N= -2.
21	+T= 16;	704	Off;	1;	1;	Any_Number;	N= -2.1
22	+T= 16;	704	Off;	1;	1;	Any_Number;	N= -2.14
23	+T= 16;	704	Off;	1;	1;	Any_Number;	N= -2.141
24	+T= 16;	704	Off;	1;	1;	Any_Number;	N= -2.1415
25	+T= 16;	704	Off;	1;	1;	Any_Number;	N= -2.14159
26	−F= 16;	705	On;	1;	13;	Ignore;	N=
27	−F= 18;	706	On;	12;	13;	Ignore;	N=
28	−F= 17;	707	On;	1;	13;	Save_Disp;	N=
29	−F= 19;	900	On;	11;	13;	Ignore;	N=
30	+T= 20;	901	Off;	13;	13;	Equals;	N= -1

Total State Count 30

Appendix B – ITE Trace File

I added a trace to each state to determine how many times a state is entered. The number in the first column is an indication of the order of when a state was entered. My additions to the trace file are indicated by my initials "gem" in lower-case. The "ready" state at 6, the "begin" at 10, and the "negated1" at 20, etc. were the original positions for tracing state. In the application code, the "begin" state uses a switch with six case statements. If you count the "begin" states below, you will count six state events. This indicates that all six possible transitions were utilized before the negative sign was entered. At the bottom of the trace file, I added the e→sig definitions found in the third column followed by the actual work being done under the column title value. I subtracted the bold states because they get counted twice when the switch uses one of the case statements where there is the original trace.

	State	e→sig	Value
1,	gem-calc,	0	
2,	gem-calc,	0	
3,	gem-calc,	1	
4,	gem-ready,	0	
5,	gem-ready,	2	
6,	**ready**		
7,	gem-ready,	1	
8,	gem-begin,	0	
9,	gem-begin,	2	
10,	**begin**		
11,	gem-begin,	1	
12,	gem-begin,	1107	
13,	gem-negated1,	0,	0
14,	gem-begin,	0	
15,	gem-calc,	0	
16,	gem-begin,	3	
17,	gem-ready,	3	
18,	gem-ready,	0	
19,	gem-negated1,	2,	0
20,	**negated1**		
21,	gem-negated1,	1,	-0
22,	gem-negated1,	1010,	-0
23,	gem-int1,	0,	-3
24,	gem-negated1,	0,	-3

25,	gem-Oper1,	0,	-3
26,	gem-calc,	0	
27,	gem-negated1,	3,	-3
28,	gem-Oper1,	2,	-3
29,	Oper1		
30,	gem-int1,	2,	-3
31,	**int1**		
32,	gem-int1,	1,	-3
33,	gem-int1,	1101,	-3
34,	gem-frac1,	0,	-3.
35,	gem-int1,	0,	-3.
36,	gem-int1,	3,	-3.
37,	gem-frac1,	2,	-3.
38,	**frac1**		
39,	gem-frac1,	1,	-3.
40,	gem-frac1,	1010,	-3.
41,	gem-frac1,	1010,	-3.1
42,	gem-frac1,	1010,	-3.14
43,	gem-frac1,	1010,	-3.141
44,	gem-frac1,	1010,	-3.1415
45,	gem-frac1,	1107,	-3.14159
46,	gem-Oper1,	1107,	-3.14159
47,	gem-frac1,	3,	-3.14159
48,	gem-opEntered,	0,	-3.14159
49,	gem-Oper1,	0,	-3.14159
50,	gem-Oper1,	3,	-3.14159
51,	gem-opEntered,	2,	-3.14159
52,	**opEntered**		
53,	gem-opEntered,	1,	-3.14159
54,	gem-opEntered,	1107,	-3.14159
55,	gem-negated2,	0,	0
56,	gem-opEntered,	0,	0
57,	gem-opEntered,	3,	0
58,	gem-negated2,	2,	0
59,	**negated2**		
60,	gem-negated2,	1,	-0
61,	gem-negated2,	1010,	-0
62,	gem-int2,	0,	-2
63,	gem-negated2,	0,	-2
64,	gem-Oper2,	0,	-2
65,	gem-calc,	0	
66,	gem-negated2,	3,	-2
67,	gem-Oper2,	2,	-2
68,	**Oper2**		
69,	gem-int2,	2,	-2
70,	**int2**		
71,	gem-int2,	1,	-2
72,	gem-int2,	1101,	-2

73,	gem-frac2,	0,	-2.
74,	gem-int2,	0,	-2.
75,	gem-int2,	3,	-2.
76,	gem-frac2,	2,	-2.
77,	**frac2**		
78,	gem-frac2,	1,	-2.
79,	gem-frac2,	1010,	-2.
80,	gem-frac2,	1010,	-2.1
81,	gem-frac2,	1010,	-2.14
82,	gem-frac2,	1010,	-2.141
83,	gem-frac2,	1010,	-2.1415
84,	gem-frac2,	1102,	-2.14159
85,	gem-Oper2,	1102,	-2.14159
86,	gem-frac2,	3,	-2.14159
87,	gem-result,	0,	-2.14159
88,	gem-Oper2,	0,	-2.14159
89,	gem-ready,	0,	-2.14159
90,	gem-calc,	0,	-2.14159
91,	gem-Oper2,	3,	-2.14159
92,	gem-ready,	2,	-2.14159
93,	**ready** ,		-2.14159
94,	gem-result,	2,	-2.14159
95,	**result**,		-2.14159
96,	gem-eval,	1104,	-2.14159
97,	gem-result,	1	-1
98,	gem-result,	100	-1
99,	gem-ready,	100	-1
100,	gem-calc,	100	-1
101,	gem-result,	3	-1
102,	gem-ready,	3	-1
103,	gem-final,	0	-1
104,	gem-calc,	0	-1
105,	gem-calc,	3	-1
106,	gem-final,	2	-1
107,	gem-final,	1	-1

e→sig definitions

IDC_1_9	1010	// the numbers one through nine
IDC_POINT	1101	// the decimal point
IDC_EQUAL	1102	// the equal sign
IDC_MINUS	1104	// the negate or minus sign
IDC_OPER	1107	// operand entered
IDC	0	

```
Q_INIT_SIG     1
Q_ENTRY_SIG    2
Q_EXIT_SIG     3
```

STATE	COUNT
ITE-States	13
gem-Calc	10
gem-Ready	9
gem-Begin	6
gem-Negated1	6
gem-Int1	6
gem-Oper1	5
gem-Frac1	10
gem-OpEntered	6
gem-Negated2	6
gem-Int2	6
gem-Oper2	5
gem-Frac2	10
gem-Result	5
gem-Eval	1
gem-Final	3

```
Total 107
       -12 ITE removed because these would be counted twice.
        95 state transitions in the ITE
```

Appendix C – COSA State Diagram

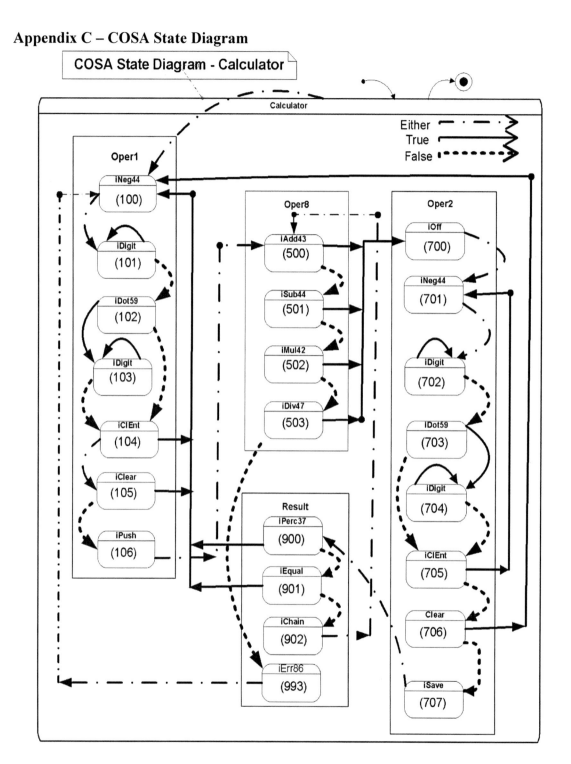

Appendix D – ITE State Diagram

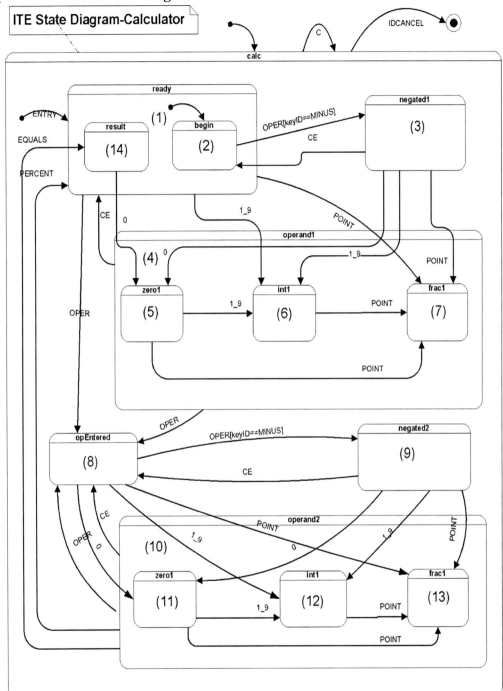

Appendix E – COSA Call Diagram

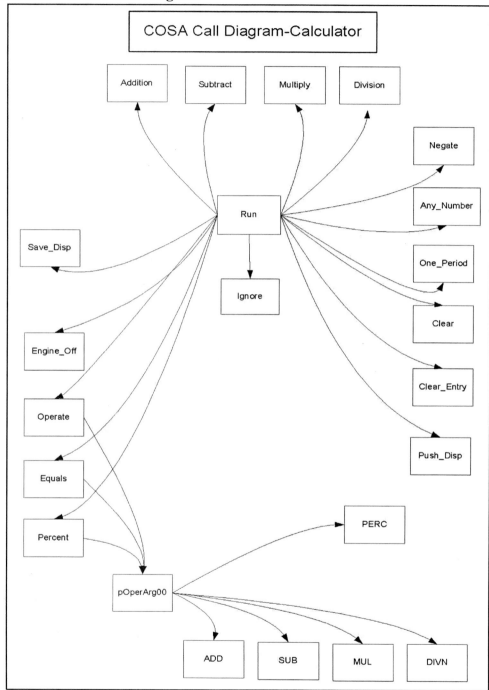

Appendix F – ITE Call Diagram

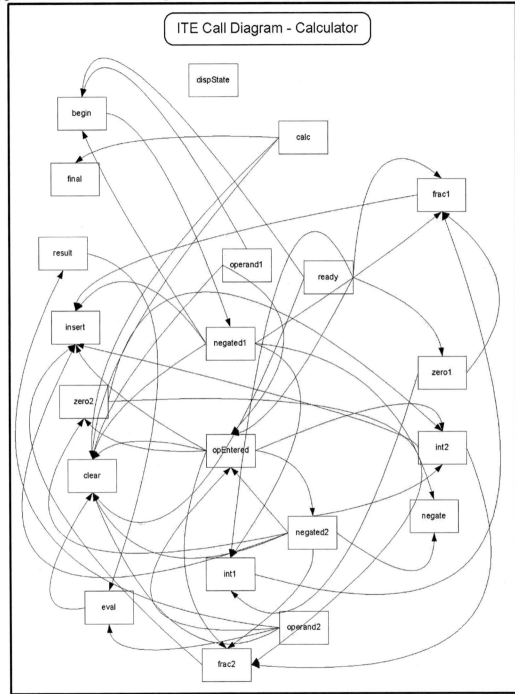

175

Appendix G – COSA Call Trace

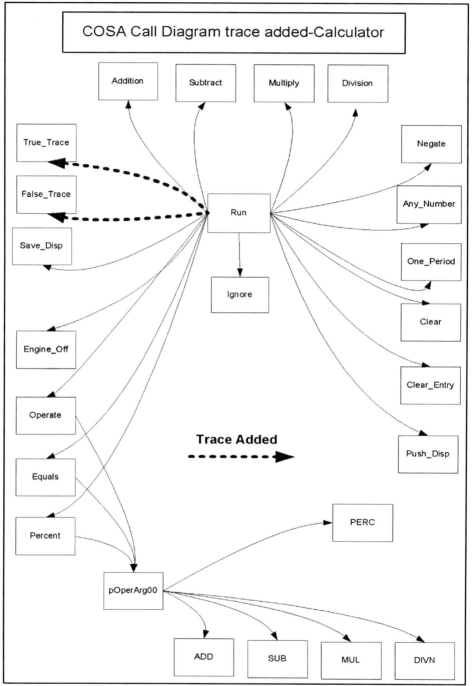

Appendix H – ITE Call Trace

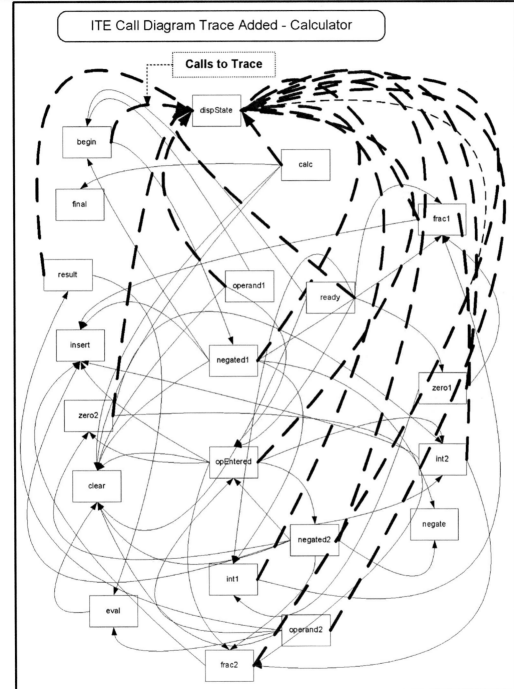

ITE Call Diagram Trace Added - Calculator

Calls to Trace

Appendix I - COSA State Diagram with Behaviors

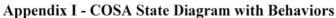

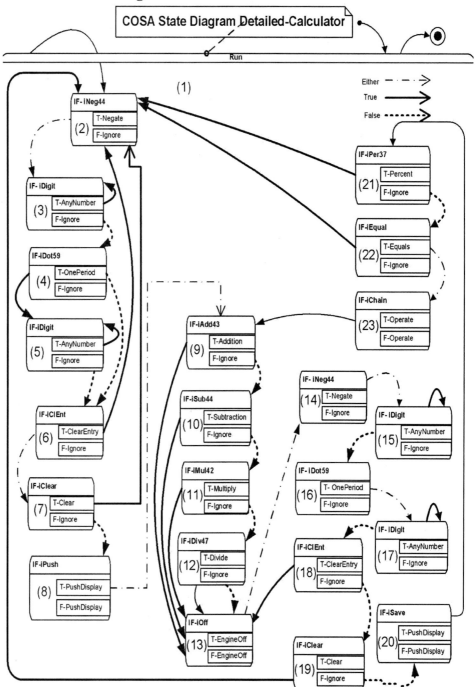

Appendix J – C++ Calculator Implementation

```cpp
//************** C++ Implementation ***********************
void aCalc::Run(int iState, LPCTSTR sDisplay) {
    sNumber = sDisplay;
    engCalc = 1;
    dynamicState = iState;
    while(engCalculate && engCalc){      //Local/Global preemption
      if(dynamicState == Tbl[iTime].state){
            COSA_Trace(iTime);
            (this->*(Tbl[iTime].True_Behavior))();
            iTime = Tbl[iTime].Next_True;
      } else {
            COSA_Trace(-iTime);
            (this->*(Tbl[iTime].False_Behavior))();
            iTime = Tbl[iTime].Next_False;
      }
    }
    pEditWnd->SetWindowText(_T(sBuildNumber));
}
```

```
//*************************** C++ Implementation ***********************
// Calculator Table
struct aCalc::aCalc_Tbl Tbl[] = { // statically build rules in table
//   Next   Next
//   True   True  False  False
//   Rule   State Behavior  Rule  Behavior  Rule  Trace
{ca(rOpr1,  iNeg44, &aCalc::Negate,    rOpr1+1,&aCalc::Ignore,   rOpr1+1,0)},
{ca(rOpr1+1,iAnyNum,&aCalc::AnyNumber,rOpr1+1,&aCalc::Ignore,   rOpr1+2,1)},
{ca(rOpr1+2,iDot59, &aCalc::OnePeriod,rOpr1+3,&aCalc::Ignore,   rOpr1+4,2)},
{ca(rOpr1+3,iAnyNum,&aCalc::AnyNumber,rOpr1+3,&aCalc::Ignore,   rOpr1+4,3)},
{ca(rOpr1+4,iClEnt, &aCalc::ClearEntry,rOpr1, &aCalc::Ignore,   rOpr1+5,4)},
{ca(rOpr1+5,iClear, &aCalc::Clear,     rOpr1, &aCalc::Ignore,   rOpr1+6,5)},
{ca(rOpr1+6,iAny,   &aCalc::PushDisp,  rOpr1, &aCalc::PushDisp,rOpr8,6)},
// operations
{ca(rOpr8,  iAdd43, &aCalc::Addition,  rOpr2, &aCalc::Ignore,   rOpr8+1,7)},
{ca(rOpr8+1,iSub44, &aCalc::Subtract,  rOpr2, &aCalc::Ignore,   rOpr8+2,8)},
{ca(rOpr8+2,iMul42, &aCalc::Multiply,  rOpr2, &aCalc::Ignore,   rOpr8+3,9)},
{ca(rOpr8+3,iDiv47, &aCalc::Division,  rOpr2, &aCalc::Ignore,   rOpr2, 10)},
// next number
{ca(rOpr2,  iAny,   &aCalc::EngOff,    rOpr2+1,&aCalc::EngOff,   rOpr2+1,11)},
{ca(rOpr2+1,iNeg44, &aCalc::Negate,    rOpr2+2,&aCalc::Ignore,   rOpr2+2,12)},
{ca(rOpr2+2,iAnyNum,&aCalc::AnyNumber,rOpr2+2,&aCalc::Ignore,   rOpr2+3,13)},
{ca(rOpr2+3,iDot59, &aCalc::OnePeriod,rOpr2+4,&aCalc::Ignore,   rOpr2+5,14)},
{ca(rOpr2+4,iAnyNum,&aCalc::AnyNumber,rOpr2+4,&aCalc::Ignore,   rOpr2+5,15)},
{ca(rOpr2+5,iAny,   &aCalc::SavDsp,    rOpr2+6,&aCalc::SavDsp,   rOpr2+6,16)},
// clear
{ca(rOpr2+6,iClEnt, &aCalc::ClrEntr,   rOpr2+1,&aCalc::Ignore,   rOpr2+7,17)},
{ca(rOpr2+7,iClear, &aCalc::Clear,     rOpr1, &aCalc::Ignore,   rResu, 18)},
// equals
{ca(rResu,  iPer37, &aCalc::Percent,   rOpr1, &aCalc::Ignore,   rResu+1,19)},
{ca(rResu+1,iEqual, &aCalc::Equals,    rOpr1, &aCalc::Ignore,   rResu+2,20)},
{ca(rResu+2,iAny,   &aCalc::Operate,   rOpr8, &aCalc::Operate, rOpr8, 21)},
{ca(rErr,   iErr86, &aCalc::Unknown,   rOpr1, &aCalc::Error,   rOpr1, 22)}
}; // end of static build
//*************************** C++ Implementation ***********************
       #define ca(r,s,t,nt,f,nf,t) r,s,t,nt,f,nt,t,
```

180

```
//--------------------------------------------------------
//Filename        Author          Date          -
//aCalculate.h    Gordon Morrison 23 June 2008   -
//--------------------------------------------------------

#ifndef aCALCULATE_H
#define aCALCULATE_H
#include "aAReadMe.h"

#include <io.h>

class aCalc {
public:
// INTERFACE
        aCalc(int iState, LPCTSTR csFilename);
        aCalc();
        ~aCalc();    // normally virtual....
// INTERFACE
private:
        int engCalculate, engCalc;
        int iTime, dynamicState;
        float fNumber, fDisplay;
        CWnd  *pEditWnd;
        CWnd  *pListWnd;
        CString    sBuildNumber, sNumber, sDisplay;
        char  cDisplay[32];

public:
        aCalc(CWnd*, CWnd*);
        int   trfl;// trace file
        CString    csTrcFilename;
        void aCalc::Run(int, LPCTSTR);
        void COSA_Trace(int);
        typedef void (aCalc::*arg0)(void);
        arg0 pOperArg00;
        struct aCalc_Tbl {
                int    ord;
                int    state;
                arg0   True_Behavior;
                int    Next_True;
                arg0   False_Behavior;
                int    Next_False;
                long   rule;
        };

public:
// Calculate Engine Methods because they are initialized in public
   void Error();
```

```cpp
        void Ignore();
        void Clear();
        void Clear_Entry();
        void Any_Number();
        void Push_Disp();
        void One_Period();
        void Engine_Off();
        void Save_Disp();
        void Negate();
        void Done();
                    void ADD();
                    void SUB();
                    void MUL();
                    void DIVN();
                    void PERC();
        void Addition();
        void Subtraction();
        void Multiply();
        void Division();
        void Percent();
        void Operate();
        void Equals();
        void Unknown();
public:

//*****************************************************************
// Insert the following code to user cosa trace!
// NOTE: When DBG is not defined no code is generated in the Engine
//
//#define DBG
//#if defined DBG
//#define xxxxx_Trace(x) COSA_Trace x
//#else
//#define xxxxx_Trace(x)
//#endif
};

#endif
```

```cpp
//-------------------------------------------------------
//    Filename          Author          Date        -
//    dCalculate.cpp    Gordon Morrison 4 April 08   -
//-------------------------------------------------------
#include "stdafx.h"
#include <stdio.h>
#include <fcntl.h>
#include <stdlib.h>
#include <io.h>
#include <sys\stat.h>
#include "aCalculate.h"
#include "sCalculate.h"
void aCalc::Error(){
}
void aCalc::Ignore(){
}
void aCalc::Clear(){
     sDisplay.Empty();
     engCalculate = 0;
     dynamicState = 1;
     sBuildNumber.Empty();
}
void aCalc::Clear_Entry(){
     sDisplay.Empty();
     engCalculate = 0;
     dynamicState = 1;
     sBuildNumber.Empty();
}
void aCalc::Any_Number(){
     sBuildNumber = sBuildNumber + sNumber;
     engCalculate = 0;
}
void aCalc::Push_Disp(){
}
void aCalc::One_Period()
     engCalculate = 0;
     sBuildNumber = sBuildNumber + '.';
}
void aCalc::Engine_Off(){
     engCalculate = 0;
}
void aCalc::Save_Disp(){
     dynamicState = 86;
}
void aCalc::Negate(){
     sBuildNumber = '-';
     engCalculate = 0;
}
```

```
void aCalc::Done(){
}
void aCalc::ADD(){
    fNumber = fNumber + fDisplay;
}
void aCalc::SUB(){
    fNumber = fNumber - fDisplay;
}
void aCalc::MUL(){
    fNumber = fNumber * fDisplay;
}
void aCalc::DIVN(){
    fNumber = fNumber / fDisplay;
}
void aCalc::PERC(){
    fNumber = fNumber * (1.0 + fDisplay/100.0);
}
void aCalc::Addition(){
    pOperArg00 = &aCalc::ADD;
    fNumber = atof(sBuildNumber);
    sBuildNumber = '\0';
    dynamicState = 1;
}
void aCalc::Subtraction(){
    pOperArg00 = &aCalc::SUB;
    fNumber = atof(sBuildNumber);
    sBuildNumber = '\0';
    dynamicState = 1;
}
void aCalc::Multiply(){
    pOperArg00 = &aCalc::MUL;
    fNumber = atof(sBuildNumber);
    sBuildNumber = '\0';
    dynamicState = 1;
}
void aCalc::Division(){
    pOperArg00 = &aCalc::DIVN;
    fNumber = atof(sBuildNumber);
    sBuildNumber = '\0';
    dynamicState = 1;
}
void aCalc::Percent(){
    pOperArg00 = &aCalc::PERC;
    fDisplay = atof(sBuildNumber);
    sBuildNumber = '\0';
    dynamicState = 1;
    try {
        pOperArg00;
```

```
                sprintf(cDisplay,"%g", fNumber);
                sBuildNumber = cDisplay;
        }
        catch (float fNumber) {
                engCalculate = 0;
                dynamicState = 86;
        }
    }
void aCalc::Operate(){
        fDisplay = atof(sBuildNumber);
        sBuildNumber = '\0';
        try {
        (this->*(pOperArg00))();
                sprintf(cDisplay,"%g", fNumber);
                sBuildNumber = cDisplay;
        }
        catch (float fNumber){
                engCalculate = 0;
                dynamicState = 86;
        }
}
void aCalc::Equals(){
        fDisplay = atof(sBuildNumber);
        sBuildNumber = '0';
   try{
                (this->*(pOperArg00))();
                sprintf(cDisplay,"%g", fNumber);
                sBuildNumber = cDisplay;
        }
        catch (float fNumber){
                pEditWnd->SetWindowText(_T("Divide by Zero."));
        dynamicState = 86;
        }
        pOperArg00 = Ignore;
        fNumber = 0.0;
        engCalculate = 0;
}
void aCalc::Unknown(){
}
```

Appendix K

What is a silver bullet?

Before we can define this term there is another term used in the computer industry that may cloud the issue of defining a silver bullet called the "killer app". The software industry is known for claims of a super application ("killer app") that will do everything and pay for itself in very little time. But rarely do these applications turn out to be as good as their claims. Wikipedia defines "killer app" as:

"A killer application (commonly shortened to "killer app") is computer jargon for software which is revolutionary and popular. A killer application may be a video game, web application, desktop application, etc."

Since there are no standard definitions for what constitutes a "killer app". The definition is left up to the market. If a standards committee were to exist for "killer apps" the committee would need to consider the definition by the application's place in time, factoring in marketing hype, a specific market, and the application's popularity within that market.

The silver bullet

A silver bullet on the other hand is a technology used by technologist. Therefore, its definition will be similar but internal to any application. There are mythical claims that a silver bullet technology will replace existing technologies with vast far-reaching improvements. Wikipedia defines silver bullet as:

186

"The metaphor of the silver bullet applies to any straightforward solution perceived to have extreme effectiveness. The phrase typically appears with an expectation that some new technology or practice will easily cure a major prevailing problem."

Actually that sounds rather reasonable like something that should occur on a fairly regular basis. The transistor is an example of a technological silver bullet. The transistor dramatically changed the world we live in. There are many examples of hardware technologies that would be consisted silver bullets. But the problem is that these views are with twenty-twenty hindsight. Look at how hardware technology advanced into the super dense integrated circuits. The silver bullet aspect of this technology is taken for granted because Moore's law told us what to expect.

On the software side of computer technology, FORTRAN was clearly a silver bullet over binary and assembly language. But now there is a problem. Software does not have a Moore's law. That's not to say that software has not had impressive gains, because it has. What would a Moore's law for software look like if it existed?

1) The applications would have to decrease in size and increase in performance and reliability.

2) Applications would have to decrease in complexity and increase in features.

3) Applications would have to be easier to trace, debug, and validate as correct.

4) Reuse on all aspects of the engineered software would have to increase.

5) The architecture would have to fit seamlessly into a Model Drive Architecture.

References

The Object-Oriented Thought Process, Matt Weisfeld, Second Edition, Developers Library, Copyright © 2004 Sams Publishing

Practical Statecharts in C/C++, Dr. Miro Samek, Copyright © 2002 CPM Books, www.cpmbooks.com

"Making model-based code generation work," Dr Juha-Pekka Tolvanen, Embedded Systems Europe, August/September 2004, www.embedded.com/europe

Parsing Techniques, Dick Grune, Ceriel J.H. Jacobs, Amstelveen/Amsterdam, July 1990/ September 1998

"UML Products by Company," Copyright © 1999-2005 Objects by Design Website

The Mythical Man-Month, Frederick P. Brooks, Jr., Copyright © 1995, Addison-Wesley Publishing Company

Visual Language, Global Communications for the 21st Century, Robert E Horn, Copyright 1998, MacroVu

The Order of Things: *How Everything in the World is Organized into Hierarchies, Structures, and Pecking Orders*, Barbara Ann Kipfer, Copyright 1998, Random House, Inc.

Open Modeling Language (OML) Reference Manual, Donald Firesmith, Brian Henderson-Sellers, Ian Graham, Copyright 1998, SIGS Reference Library

A Verilog HDL Primer, Second Edition, J. Bhasker, Copyright © 1999, Lucent Technologies

Code Complete Second Edition, Steve McConnell, Copyright © 2004, Microsoft Press.

Index

Printed in the United States
142470LV00006B/1/P